Who are the Heirs
of the Abrahamic Covenant?

Who are the Heirs
of the Abrahamic Covenant?

JOHN P. DAVIS

Foreword by Fred Klett

RESOURCE *Publications* · Eugene, Oregon

WHO ARE THE HEIRS OF THE ABRAHAMIC COVENANT?

Resource Publications
An Imprint of Wipf and Stock Publishers
199 W. 8th Ave., Suite 3
Eugene, OR 97401

www.wipfandstock.com

PAPERBACK ISBN: 978–1-6667–3102–6
HARDCOVER ISBN: 978–1-6667–2309–0
EBOOK ISBN: 978–1-6667–2310–6

JANUARY 7, 2022 9:41 AM

Contents

Foreword

THERE IS AN OLD TALMUDIC STORY about two famous rabbis, Hillel and Shammai. Shammai was approached by a gentile and asked if the rabbi could teach him the whole Torah while standing on one foot. The rabbi, known for his strict demeanor, promptly threw the man out. Rabbi Hillel, known for his more irenic personality, stood on one foot and said: "What is hateful to you, do not do to your neighbor. That is the whole Torah, the rest is commentary." I have always taught, that if I were asked for a summary of the whole Bible, I would answer: "Creation under blessing, sin bringing the curse, and then restoration of blessing, ultimately through the Messiah." There are many other ways this could be put, of course. "Paradise lost, paradise regained" would be another. Rabbi Saul of Tarsus, also known as the Apostle Paul, put it this way: "Christ redeemed us from the curse of the law by becoming a curse for us— for it is written, 'Cursed is everyone who is hanged on a tree' —so that in Christ Jesus the blessing of Abraham might come to the Gentiles, so that we might receive the promised Spirit through faith." (Galatians 3:13–14) According to Paul the Messiah is the "Last Adam" who restored what was lost by the first. (1 Corinthians 15:45)

The promise given to Abraham in Genesis 12, as John Davis rightly points out, must be seen in light of the preceding 11 chapters of the book. In fact, it must be understood in the context of the whole Bible and the overarching purpose of God revealed in Scripture. In this modestly sized jewel of a theological survey, the author takes us through the various approaches that have been made to the Abrahamic promise. He provides an extremely helpful overview of the issues involved, the various points of view that have been put forward by those from the sundry theological schools of thought, analyzes them always with the Scriptures in view, and brings us to his conclusion of the matter.

I heartily recommend this work for both the professional theologian and the educated layman eager to understand God's Word deeper and more comprehensively.

Rev. Fred Klett,
PCA Evangelist to Jewish People,
founder of the CHAIM ministry,
Pastor of the Rock of Israel PCA church plant.

Preface

As a young Christian I was nurtured in a church that approached the Bible with a dispensational hermeneutic. The Bible was revered as the Word of God. The pastor was a diligent student of Scripture. I appreciate that early influence of expository Bible teaching that God used to transform my mind and my life in so many ways.

As a new follower of Christ, I soaked in everything that I could. I memorized Scripture, studied my Bible faithfully, and read every good evangelical book that was given to me. I accepted the dispensational teaching of separate programs for both Israel and the church, and the sequence of the rapture, the tribulation, the Second Coming, and the Millennium, followed by the New Heaven and New Earth.

I am not sure back then, if I even knew the word "hermeneutic." We interpreted the Word of God literally, or at least we thought we did. I continued with that approach to the Bible at a Christian university and at a seminary that affirmed those dispensational ideals.

In my early years as a pastor, I preached mostly from the New Testament. When I did preach the Old Testament, it was mainly the use of stories for moral principles or preaching from the poetical books for devotional challenges. After about ten years of pastoring, I realized my neglect of the Old Testament and my difficulty in teaching it as a Christian book. I decided to go to Westminster Seminary for a ThM in Old Testament. One of the driving forces attracting me to Westminster was Dr. Bruce Waltke who was teaching there. I had read many of his books and was hungry to learn more of the Hebrew language and the Old Testament Scriptures.

My first course at Westminster was Hermeneutics with Dr. Vern Poythress. I had studied hermeneutics in both the university and seminary, but this time it was different. At first, I was overwhelmed and uncomfortable. As I listened to Dr. Poythress, I began to realize how much of me was in my interpretation and preaching of the text. The first paper I wrote for Dr. Poythress was on 2 Thessalonians 2. I pretty much gave a straightforward, dispensational interpretation of the text. I was used to getting "A's" most of the time during my educational years. I did not receive an "A." Instead on the back of my paper there were two pages of gentle, but thorough handwritten critiques that tore my paper to shreds. At the end of his comments Dr. Poythress wrote, "John, don't be discouraged. You will get accustomed to the expectations here at Westminster." I went on to discover that those expectations included being willing to surrender all of my pre-understanding of Scripture to a thorough exegesis of the text.

At WTS Dr. Bruce Waltke was my adviser, and he, knowing my dispensational background, suggested that I write my thesis on "A Critique of the Dispensational Understanding of the Abrahamic Covenant." I accepted his recommendation, not knowing at the time, that my study of the text, undergirded by a broader Christ-centered hermeneutic, would lead me out of dispensationalism. This short book reflects my ThM thesis, though my understanding of the Abrahamic Covenant today goes beyond my thesis of 1990.

Whether you are a dispensationalist, covenant theologian, or something else, I hope this book will at least convince you that if you are in Christ, you then are in union with the quintessential seed of Abraham, and being in union with that Seed who inherits the promise to Abraham, you are a full heir of that Covenant.

John P. Davis

Chapter 1

An Exegesis of the Abrahamic Covenant

THE BIBLICAL CONTEXT OF THE COVENANT

The Abrahamic Covenant, couched in the setting of the Pentateuch, furnishes for that body of Scripture its theme,[1] as well as
providing a theological track for the balance of Scriptures. In its
literary context the Abrahamic covenant follows on the heels of
the Babel account and is intricately tied to it. At a time of ethnic,
social, economic, and linguistic unity mankind cooperated in an
effort to achieve what appears to be " . . . security through city
building . . . and the perpetuation of his generation . . . through
monumental works of architecture."[2]

Babel was a search for a society with man at its center, not
God. In a world that was to be a God-directed world, this was an

1. David J. A. Clines suggests this theme of the books of Moses: " . . . the
partial fulfillment—which implies also the partial non-fulfillment—of the
promises to the patriarchs. The promise or blessing is both the divine initiative
in a world where human initiatives always lead to disaster, and a re-affirmation
of the primal divine intentions for man" (Clines, *The Theme of the Pentateuch*,
29).

2. Dumbrell, *Covenant and Creation*, 59–60.

arrogant human assertion.[3] As Dumbrell aptly observes concerning the dispersion: "The severity of the divine action would lead us to suppose that a gross and flagrant act of rebellion by mankind had been committed at Shinar."[4]

Instead of destroying the world as in Noah's day, God, having dispersed the world's population, now designs to reach them by graciously selecting and favoring Abraham and his seed with the end that the entire world would enjoy His blessing.

Accepting Genesis 1–11 as the background for the Abrahamic covenant, the covenant, according to Dumbrell, provides " . . . a theological blueprint for the redemptive history of the world, a redemptive history which the call of Abraham sets in train."[5] McComiskey concurs:

> [The promise given to Abraham] . . . comprises the heart of Biblical teaching regarding the people of God, for, besides affirming God's intent to form such a people, it serves to define the nature of that people in broad categories. The promise thus provides a theological continuum that spans all time.[6]

Peter J. Gentry and Stephen J. Wellum concur in their attempt to form a bridge between covenant theology and dispensationalism. In their excellent work entitled *Kingdom Through Covenant*, they demonstrate the connection between the Abrahamic Covenant and God's original purposes in creation. In their discussion of Romans 4:16–17, they come to this conclusion regarding the statement in verse 17, ". . . God . . . calls into existence the things which do not exist."

> Therefore, according to the New Testament, as we read Genesis 12–25, we are to view the call of Abraham as a kind of 'new creation.' Just as the divine word in Genesis 1:3 brings into being things that are not, so in Genesis

---

3. Dumbrell, *Covenant and Creation*, 61.

4. Dumbrell, *Covenant and Creation*, 59.

5. Dumbrell. *Covenant with Abraham*, 46.

6. McComiskey *Covenants of Promise*, 58.

12:3 it is the divine word that brings into existence a new order out of the chaos resulting from the confusion and curse of Babel – the condition of the world just prior to Genesis 12.[7]

A SURVEY OF THE COVENANT TEXTS

Genesis 12:1–3 introduces God's purposes with Abraham as "promise."[8] The first four prefix conjugations in verses 2 and 3 are all cohortatives,[9] denoting Yahweh's resolve:[10] "I will make you into a great nation"; "I will bless you"; "I will make your name great"; "I will bless those who bless you." The one non-perfective, "I shall curse the one who treats you lightly" signifies a contingent future.[11] The conjunctive vav preceding the cohortative signifies either purpose or result (in order that) after the imperative,"go".[12] [13] The combined sense is: "Yahweh said to Abram, "Go . . . to the land I will show you *that* I may make you into a great nation, *that* I may bless you, *that* I may make your name great." The imperative with waw conjunctive signifies that these divine resolves have the further purpose that Abram "be a blessing." A similar construction is found in Ruth 4:11: "May Yahweh make the woman who is entering your house like Rachel and Leah . . . and so do valiantly in Israel." The first person cohortative and non-perfective of 12:3 give the purpose\result of Abram's becoming a blessing. "Bless" signifies "to fill with life and victory" and "be" has its active sense, "become." God filled Abram with life that he in turn might mediate

---

7. Gentry and Wellum, *Kingdom through Covenant*, 225.

8. P. D. Miller Jr's syntactic study of this passage is helpful (Miller, *Vetus Testamentum*, 472–76).

9. Waltke and O'Connor, *Biblical Hebrew*, 34.1d.

10. Waltke and O'Connor, *Biblical Hebrew*, 34.5.1a.

11. Waltke and O'Connor, *Biblical Hebrew*, 31.6.2.

12. Waltke and O'Connor, *Biblical Hebrew*, 34.6.

13. Yarchin adequately defends the command\promise structure of Genesis 12:1–3 (Yarchin, *Biblical Theology,* 164–178).

life to others. As Abraham became a blessing, verse 3 describes how God fulfilled His purpose of bringing blessing to others.

Though the land promise becomes an important focus of the covenant, it is significant that it is originally set apart from God's initial promises to Abraham. The idea of land is introduced in 12:1, but the concept of land as "gift" "Land" is introduced upon Abraham's obedience and apart from the promise (see Gen 12:7).

The additional promise, "and all peoples on earth will be blessed through you," contrary to the translation in the New International Version, wherein "bless" is taken as a passive, is better translated as "find for themselves a blessing."[14]

This line of the covenant delineates the universal scope of God's redemptive and restorative program for the world.

GENESIS 15

In Genesis 15:1–6 after having successfully overcome another threat to his occupation of the land, Abraham's doubt, in light of the absence of any offspring, is assuaged by divine assurance that a son will come from Abraham. Again, the innumerability of Abraham's seed is confirmed, this time being compared to the stars of heaven. This seed of Abraham, shares a corporate solidarity as indicated by the use of "seed" in the singular. This raises the question of whether faith or ethnicity provide this solidarity among the seed of Abraham.

In 15:7 Yahweh's unsolicited affirmation concerning His promise of the land provokes from Abraham a question desiring

---

14. It should be noted that barak is used in the Niphal in Gen. 12:3 and in the Hithpael in Gen. 22:18. Though the causative-reflexive sense is usually reserved for the Hithpael, it is also a legitimate scheme in the Niphal. In both texts it is best to understand barak as "get to themselves blessing" (Waltke and O'Connor, Biblical Hebrew, 390–1). Dumbrell translates the phrases as "'win for themselves a blessing'" or "'find for themselves a blessing'" (Dumbrell, Covenant and Creation, 70–1). This is contrary to Gerhard Wehmeier's conclusion that the Niphal and Hithpael are distinct in meaning (Wehmeier, Bangalore, 1–13).

assurance, "O Sovereign Lord, how can I know that I will gain possession of it" (Gen 15:8).

In response to Abraham's need of assurance, in 15:9–21 Yahweh elevates the promise of land for Abraham and his seed to the status of covenant. First Yahweh engages in a ceremony that confirms the inviolability of His covenant with Abraham and his seed. In obedience to God Abraham gathers, divides, and arranges selected animals on the ground. In the darkness of the evening, Yahweh, in a visible manifestation of Himself, passes alone through the midst of the divided animals, thereby taking upon Himself an oath of self-malediction.[15]

The significance of this ceremony lies in God's asseveration, wherein He solemnly swears death upon Himself should He fail to fulfill His promise to Abraham.[16]

This oath-taking on God's part confirms the land promise of the Abrahamic covenant as unilateral, unconditional, and inviolable. It emphasizes the importance of the gift of land in the redemptive and restorative purpose that God is fulfilling through the Abrahamic covenant.

This land promise retains a fulfilled, yet not consummated aspect. There are indications within Scripture that the land promise is fulfilled (Josh 1:13; 11:23; 21:43–45), not yet consummated (Josh 13:1–7; Ps 95; Heb 4:6–11), and yet to be consummated in a new cosmos (Heb 11:39–40).

GENESIS 17

Genesis 17 reaffirms the promise\covenant adding the rite of circumcision as the external evidence of the parents' acceptance of the covenant and their desire for the continuity of the covenant through their seed. Though Yahweh had affirmed in reference to the land in chapter 15 His commitment to keep the promise,

15. Robertson, *Christ of the Covenants*, 130.
16. Robertson, *Christ of the Covenants*, 130–1.

Genesis 17 makes it clear that receiving the benefit of His commitment is not without obligation on those who participate.

The covenant itself in this chapter is now described in terms of a gracious gift in 17:2. Verses 4 and 5 contain an additional covenant arrangement that Abraham will be the father of nations. This is ultimately fulfilled in and in the work of Christ through the Church (Matt 28:19; Rom 4:16–17; Rom 15:8–16). Also, there is included an additional note in 17:7 that a relationship exists between Yahweh and Abraham's seed.

This promise extends to the true seed of Abraham, i.e., to Isaac, not Ishmael (Gen 17:15–22) and to Jacob, not Esau (Gen 27:27–9; 28:10–15).

The gift of land is also reaffirmed in 17:8, "And I will give to you and your offspring after you the land of your sojournings."

Circumcision is then set forth as the outward sign of the covenant relationship that exists between Yahweh and Abraham and his seed in verse 10: "Every male among you must be circumcised." This rite was open also to Gentiles, the significance of which is brought out by O. Palmer Robertson:

> This absolute openness to the incorporation of Gentiles into the community of Israel has far-reaching significance affecting the interpretation of massive portions of the Old and New Testaments. Many traditions of interpretation build on an implicit assumption that God has a distinctive purpose for the racial descendants of Abraham that sets them apart from Gentiles who respond in faith and obedience to God's program of redemption. This entire hermeneutical structure begins to totter when it is realized that 'Israel' could include non-Abrahamic Gentiles just as well as ethnically related Jews.[17]

Unfortunately, though Israel maintained outward circumcision, they often lacked circumcision of the heart which is the true mark of the seed of Abraham (Rom 2:28–29).

---

17. Robertson, *Christ of the Covenants*, 154.

GENESIS 22

Genesis 22 records the willingness of Abraham to sacrifice his seed, Isaac, in obedience to the command of Yahweh. Upon this forceful demonstration of Abraham's loyalty to Yahweh, the promise\covenant is now bound with an oath in 22:16, "I will surely bless you. The oath-bound promise\covenant, employing cohortatives of resolve, reaffirms personal blessing to Abraham, the innumerability of Abraham's seed, an additional motif of victory over enemies, and blessing to the nations through Abraham's seed, The numerous seed and the victory over enemies are administrations of "to bless." Once again *barak* signifies "to confer abundant and effective life upon something . . someone."[18]

The granting of this oath-bound promise\covenant is connected to Abraham's obedience.

It is worth noticing that in the Abraham narratives (12–22), both the issues of Abraham's obedience and the blessing to the nations form an inclusio for the cycle.[19] If any conditionality is involved, as some have suggested, it is removed on the ground of Abraham's obedience.

Later both Isaac and Jacob had the covenant reiterated to them. Throughout the Pentateuch are found frequent restatements and allusions to the promise\covenant.[20]

THE SIGNIFICANT ELEMENTS OF THE COVENANT

Clines recognizes three basic elements in the promise: posterity, divine-human relationship, and land.[21] Similarly, VanGemeren identifies four areas of the promise: a seed, a land, blessing to the

---

18. Oswalt, *Theological Wordbook*, 132.

19. See Yarchin's discussion of these narratives wherein he sees imperative\promise "gauged toward the formation of a sort of framing of the whole Abraham cycle...." (Yarchin, *Biblical Theology*, 174).

20. See Clines, *Pentateuch*, 31–43.

21. Clines, *Pentateuch*, 31

patriarchs, and blessing to the nations.[22] VanGemeren's categories of blessing to the patriarchs and to the nations correspond to Clines' division of "divine-human relationship."

I have chosen to follow Clines' three-fold breakdown as a concise encapsulation of the major elements of the Abrahamic covenant and has chosen to deftly exegete those elements as found in Genesis 12:1–3,7; 13:14–17; 15; 17:1–22; 22:15–18.

The Promise of Posterity

The Abrahamic covenant often speaks of "seed." The Hebrew word *zera* and the related Greek word *sperma* present a complex concept in identifying the recipients of the Abrahamic promise. "Seed" is used at times to include the physical descendants of Abraham, those who share the faith of Abraham, whether physical seed or not, and in Galatians 3:16, Paul argues forcefully that *sperma* in the singular finds its ultimate reference to Christ as "the" offspring of Abraham.

This variegated usage produces perplexity in understanding "who are the recipients of the Abrahamic covenant?"

Part of the solution to this complexity is to understand that *sperma* and *zera* are used to describe both a singular entity as well as a collective. The promise was given to Abraham and to his seed (Genesis 12:1–3,7; 15; 17:1–22; 22:15–18), i.e. both to Isaac (27:27–29) and to Jacob (28:10–15). Both Isaac and Jacob stood representatively in the Messianic office, an office fulfilled in Jesus Christ. McComiskey notes: "The collective function of *zera* allows the writer to refer to the group or to a representative individual of the group."[23] The focus is not on the physically related *zera;* for those who are not physically related can participate in the covenant (Gen 17:9–14). The collective singular disallows any notion of "seeds," physical and spiritual. There is but one seed.

22. VanGemeren, *Progress of Redemption*, 104.

23. McComiskey, *Covenants of Promise*, 20.

The New Testament clarifies that Jesus Christ is the ideal representative seed, while those in Christ comprise the collective seed, i.e., the community of faith (Gal 3:16, 29). Isaac and Jacob cannot ultimately fulfill the promise. Only Jesus Christ can bless the earth in a final sense. The collective seed has no identity apart from their relationship to the ideal representative, Jesus Christ.

This dual concept of "individual representative" and "corporate community of faith" is essential to understanding *zera*. It appears that later in the progress of revelation the Davidic covenant expands on the royal status of the representative individual who guarantees the covenant and the New Covenant expands on the spiritual nature of the corporate community of faith who participate in that covenant.

As indicated earlier, another step in resolving the complexity of *zera* is to understand that "seed" does not equate to "physical descendants." Though Ishmael was a descendant of Abraham, he was not the seed of Abraham to whom the promise was guaranteed. Likewise, Esau was a descendant of Isaac, yet was not in the line of promise. Also, there were many who were physically seed of Abraham through Isaac and Jacob, yet who stood outside the covenant (Rom 2:28–29).

Clearly, not all of the physical *zera* of Abraham inherit the promise. Only those physical descendants bound in a unique "covenant" relationship or those non-physical "seed" who by faith enter that covenant of Abraham inherit the promise.

The unique relationship that establishes man as the true seed of Abraham is one built on a faith participation in a divinely initiated covenant.[24] O. Palmer Robertson recognizes covenant as the bond that determines relations between God and his people:

> By creation God bound himself to man in covenantal relationship After man's fall into sin, the God of all creation graciously bound himself to man again by committing himself to redeem a people to himself from

24. See O. Palmer Robertson, WTJ 42, 259–89.

lost humanity. From creation to consummation the covenantal bond has determined the relation of God to his people.[25]

Daniel P. Fuller in his discussion of the seed of Abraham concludes that since faith is the prerequisite for participation in the Abrahamic covenant by both Jew and Gentile, then " . . . faith which produces obedience, rather than physical descent, is the primary aspect of the seed of Abraham."[26] It holds true then that physically related *zera* are not guaranteed participation in the Abrahamic promise, but the promise is insured " . . . to all the people of faith throughout all ages."[27] Once again, the New Testament affirms that not all Israelites were inheritors of the promise (Rom 2:28–29) and that some of those outside Abraham's physical seed do inherit the promise (Gal 3:29).

The "seed" of Abraham are those who by faith engage The Seed, whether physically related or not. It remains for the New Testament to clarify the notion more specifically. In any case, there is no basis for a distinction between physical seed and spiritual seed in these accounts in Genesis.

The Promise of Divine\human Relationship

The promise of divine\human relationship is bound in the terms of blessing and cursing. Divine blessing extended from Abraham to Isaac to Jacob and to their seed. The presence of blessing depicted the liveliness of the relationship between God and His people. McComiskey comments regarding blessing:

> The blessing of the Abrahamic promise then connotes every aspect of God's favor, both temporal and spiritual, bestowed on the patriarchs. The emphasis seems to be primarily on the spiritual blessing of the promise. This secured a bright future for the progeny of the patriarchs

25. Robertson, *Christ of the Covenants*, 25.
26. Fuller, "Hermeneutics," 234.
27. McComiskey, *Covenants of Promise*. 17.

in a land in which they could grow to become a great nation and affirmed that, in some yet unforeseen way, the offspring would become a blessing to Gentiles.[28]

This promise of personal blessing was reaffirmed to both Isaac (Gen 26:3) and Jacob (Gen 35:9–12). That relationship was dominant as the essence of this blessing is clarified in Genesis 17:1–8 where is found:

> . . . the concept of divine-human relationship inherent in the words 'to be your God and the God of your descendants after you' (v.7)."[29]

Also, included in this divine\human relationship is the promise that Abraham's name would be great. McComiskey explains:

> It is the promise of an enhanced reputation . . . . Because of Abraham's faithfulness his name still lives today. His example of faith and his role as mediator of the promise permeate the teaching of both testaments. . . . If it were not for his obedience to God, his name probably would have been lost.[30]

Furthermore, this divine\human relationship includes the promise of blessing for those who favor Abraham and cursing for those who disfavor him. Cursing is the experience of one who curses, "the one cursing you", Abraham and his seed. Again, McComiskey offers helpful insight into *qll*:

> The word curse in the statement of the promise clearly denotes the expression of an unfavorable attitude toward Abraham. Its emphasis on treating contemptuously or regarding as unimportant defines an attitude. It is an attitude toward Abraham that deems him unworthy of attention. It regards his example of faith as not important enough to emulate. One who disregards the fact that through Abraham God is urging everyone to faith in the

---

28. McComiskey, *Covenants of Promise*, 40.
29. McComiskey, *Covenants of Promise*, 17.
30. McComiskey, *Covenants of Promise*, 40.

promise is treating Abraham contemptuously, and may expect that God will treat him or her the same way.[31]

Moreover, the promise of divine\human relationship includes, as a result, the extension of blessing to the nations of the world. This guarantees that Abraham's seed will be the mediator of blessing to the nations. By invoking in faith the name of Abraham's God, the nations of the world share in the covenant to Abraham.[32] Through the Abrahamic covenant "this rectification of curse is worldwide in scope. . . . 'All the families of the earth' may turn from the history of curse and enter that of blessing by their own historical involvement with Abram and his descendants, the blessed of Yahweh."[33]

Divine\human relationship entails responsibility for those in the covenant. Genesis 12:2 commands Abraham to be a blessing.[34] His living within covenant obligations is part of the link of bringing blessing to the nations of the world.

The Promise of Land

The land is promised to Abraham in Genesis 12:5–7 and 13:13–17, covenanted in Genesis 15:7–18, and explicated in verses 19–21. This promise of land is repeated to Isaac (Gen 26:3–4) and to Jacob (Gen 28:3, 13–15; 35:9–12). Deuteronomy 12:8–32 describes the land as " . . . a 'resting place' (menuha) and an 'inheritance' (nahala). It is the place where God will choose a site as a 'dwelling for his Name'(v.11)."[35]

Land in the Old Testament is both a physical reality as well as a theological symbol. The 2,504 uses of "land" in the Old Testament

---

31. McComiskey, *Covenants of Promise*, 41.

32. See footnote 13.

33. Yarchin, *Biblical Theology*, 172.

34. Yarchin forcibly defends the command\promise structure of Genesis 12:1–3 (Yarchin, *Biblical Theology*, 164–78).

35. McComiskey, *Covenants of Promise*, 43.

speak of its importance to theology[36]. Though God promised to Abraham a specific piece of geography, Abraham apparently understood it as more than geography (Heb 11:16, 39–40).

Theologically, land is the gift of God. Land is the place of blessing. Land is the fulfillment of promise. Land is that sphere of life where one lives out his allegiance to Yahweh. Land is that place where Yahweh uniquely chooses to dwell and to reveal Himself[37] Land is the sphere of God's kingdom activity.

The conquest under Joshua was more than just a military invasion, it was a theological event wherein the pious in Israel had their faith confirmed in God's promise to Abraham. Joshua 21:44–45 indicates that to a measure the promise was fulfilled in Joshua's day, in Solomon's day (I Kings 8:56) and in Nehemiah's day (Neh 9:7–8). However, since the land promise is eternally operative, each and every successive generation looks for the promise of rest in "land."

Concerning the land promise, some of the poetic material (ca. Prov 2:21) ". . . demonstrates the vital principle that although the promise is irrevocable in nature, its benefits are only enjoyed by those who maintain a proper relationship to God through the obedience of faith."[38] Ultimately the realization of the land promise awaits the time of the resurrection, the removal of the curse, and the restoration of all things (Rev 21–22) under the rule of God.

The prophets (cp. Zech 14:1–11) maintain an expectation that there will be, not simply a return to the land of Palestine by the seed of Abraham, but an expansion of the territorial borders of the promised land to include the world.

Land was always important to the original purpose of God for man. At creation this land included the entire earth and all its resources. Man was given dominion over this land (Gen 1:26–28). In the fall man lost this dominion.

In an act of redemptive grace, God granted to the seed of Abraham the land, then defined more narrowly (Gen 15:18–21),

---

36. Martens, God's *Design*, 1981, 97

37. Martens, God's *Design*, 242–47.

38. McComiskey, *Covenants of Promise*, 48.

as the nation of Israel was to enjoy in a microcosmic way what God intended originally and now eschatologically for the people of God (Rev 21–22). As old Israel found rest in the land of Palestine, so the Church experiences a spiritual deliverance out of the bondage of Satan's world of sin and death to inherit rest in Christ (Heb 3–4).

To New Testament believers, this "landedness" presently finds expression in their current experience with Jesus Christ (Col 1:13) as the fulfillment of the theological symbol, accompanied by an expectation, as seen in the eschatology of the Old Testament prophets and of the New Testament, that the physical reality involves an expansion of the territorial borders to include the entire earth, the New Creation, as originally intended in Genesis 1 and 2.

Whether ethnic Israel occupies the land of Palestine in a millennial kingdom or the New Creation as fulfillment of the promise to the seed of Abraham is a question built on a constricted understanding of the terms "land" and "seed." Limiting the seed of Abraham to ethnic Israel confines the land promise to Palestine. Allowing for the inclusion of all believers in the seed of Abraham coincides with the expansion of the land promise to include the new cosmos. This does not abrogate the promise to the believing physical descendants of Abraham to occupy the land of Palestine, but expands on it.

As noted earlier, McComiskey pointed out that covenant theology does not demand an abrogation of the promise of land. To him the New Testament expands the promise of land to include the whole redeemed world under the kingship of Jesus Christ.[39] He concludes his discussion saying:

> The land will belong to the people of God because it is part of the larger triumph of Christ. Perhaps the definable borders of Canaan will no longer be important under the rule of David's son, but the promise of the land as a territorial heritage need not be considered as abrogated if one approaches the promises through covenant.[40]

39. McComiskey, *Covenants of Promise*, 199–209.
40. McComiskey, *Covenants of Promise*, 208.

SUMMARY

The Abrahamic covenant is God's answer to the failures of Genesis 1–11. In those chapters the "seed" of mankind became corrupted through the fall, the "land" was cursed with a consequent loss of man's dominion over it, and the "divine-human relationship" was ruptured. The Abrahamic covenant restores to believing mankind the promise of seed, land, and divine-human relationship.

The words of Dumbrell capture the significance of that covenant:

> The covenant with Abraham is a response to the situation created by the fall, remotely, and immediately to the circumstance arising from the humanistic attempt by man to find the center of his world in himself. The aim of the Abrahamic covenant is to redress all the aberrations of Gen. 3–11. Striking as it does a note of 'land' and 'people' as concepts with which the blessings of this covenant will be bound up, it points initially to Israel's history about to unfold. Finally, however, it directs us to the political unities sought by men in Gen. 11:1–9. These will come to the 'great nation', the company of the redeemed, which will rise by commitment to the God of Abraham. The call of that patriarch began a program of redemption which aimed at full and final restoration of man and his world. It will end with a series of relationships established by which the new creation will be brought into being.[41]

41. Dumbrell, "Covenant with Abraham," 50.

Chapter 2

Evangelical Interpretations of the Abrahamic Covenant

IN THIS CHAPTER THE ROLE of the Abrahamic Covenant in dispensationalism, covenant theology, promise theology, and others will be succinctly set forth.

CLASSIC DISPENSATIONALISM

Within the framework of classic dispensational theology, the Abrahamic covenant initiates the dispensation of Promise and introduces an unconditional and eternal covenant with the physical descendants of Abraham.

The Dispensation of Promise began textually at Genesis 12:1 and ended at Exodus 19:8.

That dispensation is distinguished from the covenant itself in that the promise was conditioned on obedience and staying in the land, while the covenant itself anticipated the "seed" that should come.[1]

Classic dispensationalists normally divide the covenant into seven parts: (1) "I will make you into a great nation," fulfilled in Abraham's natural posterity in a spiritual posterity and in the seed of Ishmael; (2) "I will bless you," entailing both temporal and spiritual blessing to Abraham: (3) "make your name great," referring to a personal promise to Abraham: (4) "you will be a blessing," finding its fulfillment in Galatians 3:13–14; (5 and 6) "bless those who bless you and whoever curses you I will curse," fulfilled in the history of the dispersions of Israel; (7) "all peoples on earth will be blessed through you," containing the great evangelistic promise fulfilled in Abraham's seed, Christ.[2]

Classic dispensationalists assert that apart from the soteriological aspect of blessing in Christ, the covenant is largely one for Abraham's physical seed. Walvoord maintains: "While the Abrahamic covenant is essentially gracious and promises blessings, it deals for the most part with physical blessings and a physical seed."[3] A rigid distinction between Israel, Abraham's physical seed, and the Church, Abraham's spiritual seed, is the benchmark of classic dispensationalism.

In his discussion of what he called the "*sine qua non* of dispensationalism" Ryrie asserted:

> A dispensationalist keeps Israel and the Church distinct. . . . This is probably the most basic theological test of whether or not a man is a dispensationalist, and it is undoubtedly the most practical and conclusive.[4]

Later he concluded that "the essence of dispensationalism, then, is the distinction between Israel and the Church."[5]

1. Scofield, *Scofield Reference Bible*, 20.
2. Scofield, *Scofield Reference Bible*, 25.
3. Walvoord, "Covenant and Premillennialism," 418,
4. Ryrie, *Dispensationalism Today*, 44–45.
5. Ryrie, *Dispensationalism Today*, 47.

In his discussion of the Abrahamic covenant Dwight Pentecost reiterates the separation between physical blessings and physical seed versus spiritual blessings and spiritual seed as set forth by Scofield and Walvoord. In an attempt to demonstrate some relationship among the various covenants, Pentecost suggests that the land promises of the Abrahamic covenant are developed in the Palestinian covenant, the seed promises in the Davidic covenant, and the blessing promises in the New Covenant.[6] All of these covenants relate to Israel.

The discovery of a Palestinian covenant in Deuteronomy 30:1–10 is distinctive to dispensationalism. Feinberg in his argument against Allis's charge that dispensationalists equate " . . . being 'in the land' as the pre-condition of blessing under this covenant" responds:

> There is a failure here to recognize that ownership of the land depended upon the Abrahamic covenant, and that in perpetuity; whereas occupation of the land depended and still depends on the Palestinian covenant of Deuteronomy 28 to 30, which demands obedience as a prerequisite.[7]

This introduction of a Palestinian covenant provides an avenue of escape for dispensationalists from the some of the charges of amillennialists who allege that the Abrahamic covenant was conditional. Classic dispensationalists would say that the Palestinian covenant sets forth the conditions for temporal participation in the blessings, yet guarantees ultimate fulfillment for all of Israel.

For the classic dispensationalist the fulfillment of the Abrahamic covenant awaits an eschatological time when physical Israel is restored to their land permanently. The New Testament age does not relate to the Abrahamic covenant apart from one's faith participation in the soteriological aspect of blessing in Christ. New Testament believers in no other way fulfill or participate in the promises to the physical seed of Abraham.

6. Pentecost, *Things to Come*, 72.
7. Feinberg, *Millennialism*, 87–88.

To the classic dispensationalist the anticipated kingdom is marked by the superior position of Israel over the rest of the world wherein for one thousand years they will enjoy the unprecedented earthly blessing promised to Abraham.

Some of the more important and relatively modern treatments on the Abrahamic covenant by classic dispensationalists are those by John Walvoord,[8] the discussion by Dwight Pentecost,[9] the works by Charles Ryrie,[10] and the notes found in both the Old and New Scofield Bible.[11]

MODIFIED/PROGRESSIVE DISPENSATIONALISM

Among other things, modified dispensationalists recognize varying degrees of realized eschatology in the New Testament. In discussing the eschatological blessing promised to Israel, Robert Saucy suggests the possibility that the present experience of the Church may be "the beginning of the eschatological blessings promised for the messianic age which will be shared by all believers."[12] He views the Pentecostal gift of the Spirit, though having direct reference to Israel in the book of Joel, as participation in that new messianic age.[13]

This is definitely a "progression" in dispensational teaching. It is a tacit admission of the "already, not yet" approach to fulfillment of Old Testament prophecy. Also, modified dispensationalists see much more continuity between Israel and the Church. Though Saucy would reject " . . . a new continuity which sees the Church as a kind of new Israel which has now taken over the promises of Israel . . . ,"[14] he does adhere to a continuity of the "people of God." He explains: . . . it is perhaps best to say that the 'people of God'

8. Walvoord, The Abrahamic Covenant and Premillennialism," 414–22.

9. Pentecost, *Things to Come*, 65–94.

10. Ryrie, *Dispensationalism Today*.

11. Scofield, *The Scofield Bible*, 24–24.

12. Saucy, *Israel and the Church*, 250.

13. Saucy, *Israel and the Church*, 250.

14. Saucy, *Israel and the Church*, 241.

is one people, since all will be related to him through the same covenant salvation. But the affirmation of this fundamental unity in a relation to God through Christ does not eliminate the distinctiveness of Israel as a special nation called of God for a unique ministry in the world as a nation among nations.[15]

Robert Saucy also represents a softening of the earthly/heavenly dichotomy between Israel and the Church when he asserts:

> The earlier dispensational teaching that divided the people of God into an earthly and heavenly people (i.e., the Church and Israel), with fundamentally no continuity in the plan of God on the historical plane, must be rejected . . . .[16]

Saucy views the people of God as " . . . enlarged to include those from other nations other than Israel," though without the Church assuming that position exclusively for herself [17] This admission of unity between Israel and the Church as "people of God" marks another shift in dispensationalism. Furthermore, modified dispensationalists speak more consistently of the method of salvation. Allen P. Ross, though maintaining that the actual content of revelation for saving faith differed throughout the dispensations, sets forth Abraham as an example that salvation in both testaments is by grace through faith.[18] His closing admission that being "a covenant theologian with a dispensational hermeneutic" best describes the biblical method of salvation[19] is another tacit admission of the unity of redemption in both Testaments.

This continuity of the "people of God" sharing "the same covenant salvation" marks another alteration in dispensationalism.

Modified dispensationalists have made at least three major modifications in their theological system. They allow for a limited "already, not yet" approach to fulfillment of Old Testament

---

15. Saucy, *Israel and the Church*, 241

16. Saucy, *Israel and the Church*, 241.

17. Saucy, *Israel and the Church*, 241.

18. Ross, *Creation and Blessing*, 164–69.

19. Ross, *Creation and Blessing*, 178.

prophecy, they adhere to more of a continuity between and unity of the people of God, and they no longer maintain the rigid grace\law distinction, seeing more coherence in the history of redemption.

FORMER DISPENSATIONALISTS

The Institute for Christian Economics publishes two newsletters that challenge traditional dispensationalism.[20] A few articles argue the continuity of Israel and the Church based upon the interpretation of the olive tree in Romans 11. They also contend that Acts 15, "the most important passage in dispensationalism,"[21] is grossly misinterpreted[22] in order to develop a scheme for a future restoration of Israel.

COVENANT THEOLOGY

Covenant theology has traditionally viewed the Abrahamic covenant as an extension of the covenant of grace to insure an elect seed. It is regarded as a conditional covenant in reference to its temporal blessings to Israel. Its earthly fulfillment depended on the obedience of the physical seed.

The promise of land and numerous seed were fulfilled historically during the time of the monarchy, while the promise of

---

20. Gentry, "Dispensationalism's Achilles Head," Part s1–3, and Gilstrap, "Dispensationalism's Achilles Heel" Parts 1–3, and "The Most Important Passage in the New Testament," Parts 1–3.

21. Scofield, *Scofield Bible*, 1_69.

22. Six reasons for the invalidity of the traditional dispensational interpretation are taken from Gates, "The Amos Quotation," 20–22. The six reasons are "(1) It ignores James's identification of God's current work among the Gentiles with the Amos prophecy, (2) It attributes to James unwanted 'dispensational insight,' (3) It misinterprets 'after this,' (4) It fails to recognize in the birth of 'David's Greater Son' the rebuilding of the fallen house of David, (5) It fails to note the identification of the Gentiles of verse 14 whom Peter visited with those of verse 17 in the Amos prophecy, and (6) It fails to furnish James with adequate and relevant grounds on which to base his conclusion" (Gates quoted by Michael R. Gilstrap in "Dispensationalism in Transition," May 1969, 2).

universal blessing (salvation) is fulfilled through Christ in the Church.[23] Jesus Christ as the ultimate seed of Abraham offered perfect obedience and secured the eternal blessings of that covenant to all His people.[24]

The Church is identified as the new Israel and as heir of all the covenantal blessings. Covenant theologians hold that the Abrahamic covenant, though foreshadowed in earthly realities, was focused on the ideal eternal state of things. They would argue that Abraham understood that his " . . . expectation was by no means focused upon that which is immediately perceptible to the senses, but rather that the country he sought was not one of the earth."[25]

Fred Klooster

One modern day covenant theologian, Fred Klooster, understands the Abrahamic covenant in light of the royal grants of the Ancient Near East. Affirming the concept of "kingdom" as the interpretive key to the Bible,[26] he holds a Kingdom\Covenant Theology.[27] For him covenants are " . . . royal instruments. They are not ends in themselves, but instruments of God's larger kingdom activity."[28] This kingdom was established at the first advent of Jesus Christ, is presently experienced in the Church, and will be fully realized in the new heavens and earth.

For Kingdom\Covenant theologians the Abrahamic covenant is viewed as an everlasting covenant[29] that is fulfilled in Jesus Christ.[30] The Church " . . . is introduced, therefore, to meet the new

23. Allis, *Prophecy*, 56–8.
24. Allis, *Prophecy*, 36.
25. Hughes, *Divine Plan*, 14.
26. Klooster, *The Kingdom*, 1979.
27. Klooster, *Biblical Method*, 135.
28. Klooster, *Biblical Method* 150.
29. Klooster, *Biblical Method*, 150.
30. Klooster, *Biblical Method*,158.

situation arising from the fulfillment of the Abrahamic Covenant that brings Christ's blessings to all nations."[31]

Martin Woudstra

Another contemporary covenantal writer, Marten Woudstra, maintains that the concept of "people of God" is larger than a purely ethnic reference to Israel. In arguing for continuity between the Church and Israel, he demonstrates that there is both a line of inclusion and exclusion running through both testaments.[32] The line of inclusion is determined by what he describes as the "the undeniable center to Old Testament religion."[33]

This center, he says, " . . . lies in the believer's response to the words of the covenant God that He would be Abraham's God and the God of his descendants."[34]

Woudstra demonstrates that the Church is the Israel of God by showing that the New Testament images of the Church (i.e., bride, flock, strangers, people of God, etc.) are carried over from the Old Testament.[35]

He argues that the "saving of all Israel" in Romans 9 is presently being accomplished through the formation into one body of both Jew and Gentile and that Israel " . . . will not form a separate program or a separate entity next to the church."[36]

O. Palmer Robertson

Another covenant theologian, O. Palmer Robertson, approaches the Abrahamic covenant in its relationship to the original purpose of God to redeem a people for Himself. He sees its inauguration

31. Klooster, *Biblical Method*, 159.
32. Woudstra, *Israel and the Church*, 225.
33. Woudstra, *Israel and the Church*, 227.
34. Woudstra, *Israel and the Church*, 227.
35. Woudstra, *Israel and the Church*, 233–35.
36. Woudstra, *Israel and the Church*, 236–37.

in Genesis 15 where God alone confirms the promise by participating in a rite wherein He takes upon Himself an oath of self-malediction should the promise fail.[37] Robertson affirms that the New Covenant, which he terms "the covenant of consummation,"

> . . . superseded God's previous covenantal administrations. At the same time it brings to focal realization the essence of the various covenants experienced by Israel throughout their history.[38]

He perceives that the promises affirmed under the New covenant received a "mini-realization" in post-exilic times, a "fuller realization" in this age, and a "consummate realization" at the resurrection and restoration of the whole earth.[39]

Thomas Edward McComiskey

Thomas Edward McComiskey offers a fresh assessment of the Abrahamic covenant within covenant theology. Instead of destroying the world as in Noah's day, God designed to reach the world by graciously selecting and favoring Abraham and his seed with the end that the entire world would experience blessing.

The promise given to Abraham, according to him, is central to biblical theology. He says:

> [The promise given to Abraham] . . . comprises the heart of biblical teaching regarding the people of God, for, besides affirming God's intent to form such a people, it serves to define the nature of that people in broad categories. The promise thus provides a theological continuum that spans all time.[40]

In its reiteration in Genesis 17:1–8 McComiskey finds " . . . the concept of a divine-human relationship inherent in the

---

37. Robertson, *Covenants*, 128–31.

38. Robertson, *Covenants*, 272.

39. Robertson, *Covenants*, 288–89.

40. McComiskey, *Covenants of Promise*, 58.

words 'to be your God and the God of your descendants after you'(v.7)."[41] This relationship of faith offers the benefits of the promise to people of all ages[42] and establishes the continuity of the redeemed of both testaments.

McComiskey maintains that the Old Testament retains on the basis of the Abrahamic covenant an expectation that there will be an experience of rest and security in the land of Palestine and that the prophets added an expansion of the territorial borders to include the world.[43]

He argues that covenant theology does not demand an abrogation of the promise of land. To him the New Testament expands the promise of land to include the whole redeemed world under the kingship of Jesus Christ.[44] He concludes his discussion saying:

> The land will belong to the people of God because it is part of the larger triumph of Christ. Perhaps the definable borders of Canaan will no longer be important under the rule of David's son, but the promise of the land as a territorial heritage need not be considered as abrogated if one approaches the promises through covenant.[45]

Anthony Hoekema

Anthony Hoekema in considering the promise of land sees multiple fulfillments during Israel's history but a consummate fulfillment in the earth. The territorial borders are expanded to include the whole earth and the recipients of the promise include all the redeemed.[46] It is most important to note that by "earth" in this context he means the "new earth" of Revelation 21–22.

41. McComiskey, *Covenants*, 17.

42. McComiskey, *Covenants*, 16–17.

43. McComiskey, *Covenants*, 42–51.

44. McComiskey, *Covenants*, 199–209.

45. McComiskey, *Covenants*, 208.

46. Hoekema, *The Bible*, 206–212; 274–87.

William J. Dumbrell

Another covenant author, W. J. Dumbrell, views the Abrahamic covenant as formulating the general structure which will implement God's purposes for creation.[47] To him the covenant annuls the curse of the first eleven chapters. The covenant with Abraham " . . . began a program of redemption which aimed at full and final restoration of man and his world."[48]

Though holding a different view than McComiskey on the relationship of the covenants to his proposed Covenant of Creation, Dumbrell agrees to not spiritualize " . . . the Old Testament promises, unrealized in Israel's experience in the Old Testament, by transferring them to the people of God in the New Testament.[49]

To Dumbrell the fulfillment of the covenants is tied to the New Covenant's promise of "renewal, not only of the land, but of creation itself, to a new heaven and a new earth."[50]

Willem VanGemeren

One other Covenant theologian, Willem VanGemeren, blends both creation and redemptive theology, as well as exegetical and biblical theology. For him this integration " . . . bears witness to the unified purpose of God in Christ.[51] He concludes that the selection of Israel was not the abandoning of the nations, but rather was God means of bringing redemption to them.[52] He sees the goal of the patriarchal promise as the Lord's plan to redeem to himself a "community of peoples."[53]

VanGemeren recognizes three aspects of kingdom in the Bible: (1) God's universal kingdom over all the earth; (2) the

47. Dumbrell, *Covenant*, 64.
48. Dumbrell, *Covenant*, 50.
49. Dumbrell, *Covenant*, 184.
50. Dumbrell, *Covenant*, 185.
51 VanGemeren, *Progress of Redemption*, 52.
52. VanGemeren, *Progress of Redemption*, 78–79.
53 VanGemeren, *Progress of Redemption*, 105.

theocratic kingdom of Israel; (3) and the eschatological kingdom, inaugurated in Christ and which is both present and future.[54]

He concludes that "the goal of the kingdom is nothing less than the extension of God's rule over the earth, the sphere of his creation and redemption."[55] Though he is open to discussion concerning interpretation of the role of Israel,[56] he holds that salvation history for Israel in the Old Testament typifies universal salvation in the restoration of the heaven and earth:

> The promises, covenants, blessings, the Exodus, the giving of his Word, and the conquest of Canaan are acts of God foreshadowing the restoration of heaven and earth. What God does in Israel is, on a small scale, what he plans for all the nations The land of Canaan is a microcosm of the earth.[57]

PROMISE THEOLOGY

Walter C. Kaiser, Jr. represents an approach to Biblical theology that maintains "the promise of God" as the center. For him the Abrahamic covenant plays a major role in defining that promise. The terms of that covenant specify a seed, land, and blessing to the nations.[58]

Holding to a hermeneutical principle that only antecedent revelation can inform a text,[59] he opts for a literal fulfillment of the Abrahamic covenant that would be consistent with the way it was understood by its recipients.

54VanGemeren, *Progress of Redemption*, 348–54.

55. VanGemeren *Progress of Redemption*, 351.

56. VanGemeren in Feinberg, *Continuity and Discontinuity*, 60–61.

57. VanGemeren *Progress of Redemption*, 79.

58. Kaiser, *Old Testament Theology*, 88–91.

59. Kaiser, *Old Testament Theology*, 26.

His approach to interpretation which limits the New Testament from informing one's understanding of the Old,[60] leads him to conclude that

> . . . Yahweh made a covenant to give to Abraham and his seed the whole land. Such a material or temporal blessing was not to be torn apart from the spiritual aspects of God's great promise. Nor was it to be spiritualized or transmuted into some type of heavenly Canaan of which the earthly Canaan was only a model.[61]

Though contending for the unity of the people of God in all ages, he affirms that " . . . there yet remains an expectation of a future inheritance which will also conclude God's promises with a revived nation of Israel, the kingdom of God, and the renewed heavens and earth.[62]

For Kaiser the heart of understanding the Old Testament prophets is in how one answers three questions:

> Can the Christian still expect (1) a restoration of the Jewish people to their native land, (2) a large conversion of Jews in the future, (3) a future glorious kingdom composed of Jews and Gentiles?[63]

He answers in the affirmative to all of the above.

KINGDOM THROUGH COVENANT

As mentioned earlier, Gentry and Wellum seek to establish a bridge between covenant and dispensational theology. Gentry, a biblical theologian, and Wellum, a systematic theologian, combine their disciplines to show the importance of understanding the biblical covenants, including the Abrahamic Covenant. They propose the following:

60. Kaiser, *Old Testament Theology*, 99.
61. Kaiser, *Old Testament Theology*, 90.
62. Kaiser, *Old Testament Theology*, 26. 9.
63. Kaiser, *Old Testament Theology*, 97–8.

> Yet, given the fact that God has progressively revealed his eternal plan to us over time and through covenants, in order to discern God's plan correctly we must understand each covenant in its own redemptive-historical context by locating that covenant in relationship to what preceded it and what comes after it. When we do this, not only do we unpack God's unfolding plan, but we discover how that one plan comes to fulfillment and culmination in Christ and the inauguration of the new covenant with all its theological entailments (See Heb 1:1–3; 7:1–10:18; cf. Eph 1:9–10).[64]

In regard to the eschatological fulfillment of the land promises, Gentry and Wellum Conclude:

> The New Testament announces that the inheritance of the "land" is fulfilled in our Lord Jesus Christ, who brings to completion all of the previous covenants (along with their types and shadows) and who in his cross work inaugurates the new creation.[65]

SUMMARY

As can be seen from the preceding review, winds of change are whisking through both dispensational and covenant writings. That change will likely continue. Some critical differences remain, but the areas of conflict continue to narrow.

---

64. Gentry and Wellum, *Kingdom through Covenant*, 25.

65. Gentry and Wellum, *Kingdom through Covenant*, 713.

Chapter 3

Hermeneutical Issues in Interpreting the Abrahamic Covenant

INTRODUCTION

The hermeneutical issues in dispensationalism's understanding of the Abrahamic covenant revolve around what Ryrie has termed "the *sine qua non* of Dispensationalism."[1] Two of these aspects are (1) the distinction between Israel and the Church and (2) the normal or plain interpretation of Scripture. As will be seen, both of these are inextricably woven together.

For some, the second *sine qua non* provides the basis for determining the first.[2] Vern Poythress recognized that " . . . nearly all the problems associated with the dispensationalist-non-dispensationalist conflict are buried beneath the question of literal interpretation."[3] However, the question of "literal interpretation" receives conflicting answers from those who employ the term. Consequently, due to the difficulty of conclusively answering the

1. Ryrie, *Dispensationalism*, 43–47.
2. Ryrie, *Dispensationalism*, 97.
3. Poythress, *Dispensationalists*, 78.

question of "what is meant by literal?", progressive dispensationalists have conceded " . . . that consistently literal exegesis is inadequate to describe the essential distinctive of Dispensationalism."[4]
Saucy would agree saying that "the key distinctive of dispensational theology . . . is the recognition of Israel as a nation set apart
from other nations by God for the service of universal salvation
for all peoples."[5]

What dispensationalists traditionally called "literal interpretation" resulted in a bifurcation of the material in the two Testaments and a corollary, continuing discontinuity between Israel
and the Church. Daniel Fuller summarizes Oswald T. Allis's objec-
tion to Dispensationalism saying that the " . . . basic hermeneutical error in Dispensationalism was its insistence on dividing and
compartmentalizing the Scriptures, with the result that a most
important distinction was made between those Scriptures relating
to Israel and those relating to the Church."[6]

Progressive Dispensationalism has returned to the first *sine
qua non*, i.e., the distinction between Israel and the church, as its
"distinguishing factor."[7] This return coincides with Poythress's further recognition that this distinction is more fundamental than
a literal hermeneutic. He writes: "Their approaches toward strict
literalness seem to be subordinated to the more fundamental principle of dual destinations for Israel and the church."[8]

Strikingly, in discussing those dual destinations dispensationalists have moved away from the absolute earthly\heavenly
dualism of early dispensationalism. Early dispensationalism, as
evidenced in Darby's teaching, provided the groundwork for an
absolute distinction. Darby maintained a distinction between Israel and the Church that was both temporal and eschatological. He
propounded an earthly\heavenly dichotomy between Israel and

4. Blaising and Bock, *Dispensationalism*, 272.

5. Saucy, "Israel and the Church," 221.

6. Fuller, *Gospel and Law*, 19.

7. Blaising and Bock, *Dispensationalism*, 273 and Saucy, "Israel and the
Church," 221.

8. Poythress, *Dispensationalists*, 78.

the Church.[9] His views were followed by Lewis Sperry Chafer and others.

Nevertheless, Blaising notes that in the 1950s and 1960s dispensational writers had dropped the earthly\heavenly dualism and instead accepted that both Israel and the Church ultimately shared eternal destinies in the same sphere.[10]

Apparently among many contemporary dispensationalists there is agreement that " . . . the city of God is the common destiny of all the redeemed."[11] However, the question remains, if ultimately both share a common destiny, then wherein lies the "distinguishing factor," namely, the distinction between Israel and the Church? That distinction appears to lie in the earthly fulfillment of the land promise to national, ethnic Israel whom dispensationalists understand to be the "seed" of Abraham. For the dispensationalists, this is what "literal" hermeneutics demand. Walvoord remarks: The Old Testament saints and prophets expected a special program for the nation of Israel consummating in a kingdom era. This was the normal understanding of the promises.[12] Again, progressive dispensationalists agree:

> Thus, while there is in the present salvation in Christ a partial fulfillment of the spiritual blessing promised to all people through Abraham and his seed, many aspects of the promise remain to be fulfilled, especially those dealing with the 'great nation' seed and the 'land.'[13]

However, a plaguing issue with dispensational hermeneutics is the lack of consistency in definition and application of "what is literal", resulting in confusion. Vern Poythress highlights this problem of consistency when he asks concerning dispensationalists:

> Are they really begging the important questions? Are they really slanting the case in favor of 'flat interpretation'? Or

9. Blaising and Bock, *Dispensationalism*, 273–75.

10. Blaising and Bock, *Dispensationalism*, 276.

11. Blaising and Bock, *Dispensationalism*, 277

12. Walvoord, *Israel's Program*, 19.

13. Saucy, "Israel and the Church," 58.

are they just being imprecise? Maybe they are just imprecise, but the particular way in which they are imprecise does not help to delineate the issues separating dispensationalist from non-dispensationalist hermeneutics. It rather confuses them.[14]

LITERAL INTERPRETATION

If literal interpretation is confined to what the human author or recipient of revelation would have understood of "seed" and "land", then its application to the Abrahamic covenant would seem to result in a limitation of its scope to ethnic Israel and the land of Palestine. However, if by literal interpretation one means any meaning inherent in the words of a text even as nuanced by future revelation, then its application to the Abrahamic covenant results in a fuller understanding of "seed" and "land."

Walter Kaiser would be right in insisting that the meaning of a text can only be informed by antecedent revelation,[15] if he was referring to meaning as understood by its original recipients. Certainly, without the benefit of future revelation they could only understand in terms of what existed. However, to maintain that the recipients of later revelation are confined to the original recipient's sometimes-limited understanding of a text is too narrow.

Scalise comments in this regard:

> The history of exegesis seems generally to demonstrate that when the *sensus literalis* of Scripture has been defined in a positive and more than woodenly literal way (cf. especially Augustine and Luther), resulting in a synthesis of grammatical, historical, and theological understandings, a flourishing of the exegetical discipline and a renewal of dynamic biblical theology has recurred.[16]

---

14. Poythress, *Dispensationalists*, 94.

15. Kaiser, *Old Testament Theology*, 99.

16. Scalise, "Sensus Literalis," 65.

Scalise's point requires some amplification. As stated earlier, to limit a text's fullest interpretation to its grammatical-historical meaning is too restrictive. On the other hand, to include theological interpretation with the grammatical-historical is to allow progressive revelation to inform the text.

Berkhof asserts that grammatical-historical interpretation does not meet " . . . all the requirements for the proper interpretation of the Bible.[17] In his view grammatical-historical interpretation does not account for the following:

> (1) that the Bible is the word of God; (2) that it constitutes an organic whole, of which each individual book is an integral part; (3) that the Old and New Testament are related to each other as type and antitype, prophecy and fulfillment, germ and perfect development; (4) that not only explicit statements of the Bible, but also what may be deduced from it by good and necessary consequences, constitute the Word of God.[18]

As noted earlier, Kaiser's view that only antecedent revelation can inform a text is inadequate. Equally inadequate is a view of interpretation that limits itself to grammatical-historical meaning. Though dispensationalists have quoted Bernard Ramm to support their understanding of "literal"[19] they fail to notice that Bernard Ramm aptly affirmed that though literal interpretation " . . . is the only conceivable method of beginning and commencing to understand literature of all kinds,"[20] he also recognized the role of typology:

> The program of the literal interpretation of Scripture does not overlook the figures of speech, the symbols, the types, the allegories that as a matter of fact are to be found in Holy Scripture. It is not a blind letterism nor a wooden literalism as is so often the accusation.[21]

17. Berkhof, *Biblical Interpretation*, 133.

18. Berkhof, *Biblical Interpretation*, 133.

19. Pentecost, *Things to Come*, 9–11.

20. Ramm, *Interpretation*, 123.

21. Ramm, *Interpretation*, 126.

Theological interpretation adds another dimension to understanding the historical-grammatical meaning of Scripture. Vern Poythress defines grammatical-historical interpretation as interpretation that " . . . deals with what a passage says against the background of its original time and culture, bearing in mind the purpose of the human author."[22] He correctly concludes that what dispensationalists mean by literal is actually the grammatical-historical interpretation of a text.[23] Pentecost equates the grammatical-historical method with literal interpretation[24] as does Ryrie[25] who also charges that non-dispensationalists "introduce another hermeneutical principle (the 'theological' method) in order to have a hermeneutical basis for the system which he holds."[26]

The grammatical-historical approach to Scripture is necessary and adequate as a starting point. However, it falls short due to the now enlarged context of Scripture. It must be conceded that knowing even what Abraham understood by the words of the covenant cannot be fully arrived at from the Old Testament text itself, as is indicated by the writer of Hebrews commentary on that understanding in Hebrews 11:16: "Instead they were longing for a better country—a heavenly one." No reading of the Old Testament text alone will confirm that Abraham was looking for a heavenly city. Yet, the New Testament declares that he was. The New Testament text introduces a dimension in understanding the heavenly nature of the land that a grammatical-historical approach alone does not yield.

THEOLOGICAL CORRESPONDENCE

A related issue to the grammatical-historical-theological approach to Scripture is that of theological correspondence. Correct

---

22. Poythress, *Dispensationalists*, 97.

23. Poythress, *Dispensationalists*, 86.

24. Pentecost, *Things to Come*, 9.

25. Ryrie, *Dispensationalism*, 92–96.

26. Ryrie, *Dispensationalism*, 94.

interpretation is grounded in the recognition of continuity in the theological purpose of God. The dualism of the earthly and heavenly, of Israel and the Church, and of law vs. grace, and the bifurcation of the testaments on those bases produce a theological discontinuity. In this author's investigation of Old Testament theology, a tentative theological paradigm has been developed through which the rest of Scripture is viewed.

This paradigm for the study of Old Testament theology is set within the parameters of God's stated purpose for man as recorded in Genesis 1:26–27. An examination of this purpose discloses a two-fold, yet united, design for humanity.

Primarily, God intended for man to have relationship with Himself. The term used to describe this relationship is "Sonship." Secondly, God intended that man should be responsible to Him and responsible for His creation. This responsibility is termed "Stewardship." This "Sonship/Stewardship" motif provides an initial paradigm for the study of Old Testament Biblical Theology.

However, the fall of man, which disoriented man from fulfilling God's design, necessitates an additional motif that runs parallel to the first and that, at times, overshadows the first. From the event of the fall, there emerges a "Redemptive\Restoration" motif that continues throughout the Scripture.

It is within the parameters of God's original intent of Sonship\Stewardship, paralleled by and at times overshadowed by Redemptive\Restoration, that a paradigm for Old Testament Theology and for understanding the Abrahamic covenant is presented.

The function of covenant relates to this overarching motif. The covenant served to ensure that there would be a seed to carry forth the Sonship\Stewardship purpose of God. The covenant grows out of the Redemptive\Restoration motif.

It is the above theological basis and understanding of the unity of the purpose of God that supply certain normative features for making theological interpretations. When applied to the Abrahamic covenant, a paradigm such as this relates that covenant to the original purpose of God and establishes a unity and continuity in that purpose. As Dumbrell was previously quoted: "The call of that patriarch began a program of redemption which aimed at full and final restoration of man and his world."[27]

Theological correspondence relates the concepts of seed, land, and divine\human relationship to the original and ultimate purposes of God and thus yields more than a provincial interpretation.

AUTHORIAL INTENTION

The issue of literal interpretation also involves that of authorial intention. Most interpreters limit the scope of interpretation of the Abrahamic covenant to what Moses understood in recording those words for the nation of Israel. Since Scripture is marked by both divine and human authorship, is it necessary that the intent of the words was shared equally by both authors? Conceivably, due to the dual authorship of the Bible (Divine\human), the answer to the question of intention may be thought of as unattainable because of the absence of the Author\author.

However, since God has preserved only the words of these authors, and in those words expects men to understand the message, interpreters must conclude that the intention of the Author\ author is that which is based singularly in the words of Scripture as contained in the canon of Scripture. Any other supposed intention is not available and, therefore, not necessary to the interpretation of Scripture. Any contextual interpretation must then be based on the words found in the text.

Although having affirmed that intention is based on the textual meaning of the words, dispensationalists must yet realize that both authors did not necessarily share the same scope of intended meaning. Paul D. Feinberg in defending the hermeneutics of dispensationalism rejects any notion that there could be any difference between the human author's intentions and God's.[28] Nevertheless, though the human author's intention would not conflict

---

27. Dumbrell, "Covenant with Abraham," 50.

28. Feinberg, *Continuity*, 177.

with the divine author's, there is no necessity for it to have been coordinate with the scope of the Divine author's intention.

For instance, there are some who would hold that in Psalm 2 the human author envisioned the human Davidic king as the anointed of God, while the divine author, as is seen in the New Testament usage of Psalm 2, ultimately intended to focus on one particular Davidic king, the Messianic King. Is there contradiction? No! There is merely difference in the intended scope of the words. It is this difference in the depth and scope of intention that helps us to understand some of the New Testament uses of the Old Testament, especially in prophetic and poetic passages.

The same can be said of the Abrahamic covenant. Though the human recipient, Abraham, and the human author, Moses, may have had a provincial, limited understanding of the scope of that covenant, the latter prophets and New Testament authors share the expanded scope of the divine author.

It is also plausible that an interpreter of Scripture may underestimate what the original recipients understood. Though the Abrahamic covenant furnishes a theological justification for the conquest of Palestine by Israel, is it not possible that the Israelites also maintained an understanding of the covenant that was set against the larger backdrop of God's original and continuing purposes for all creation as recorded in Genesis 1–11? Again, Hebrews 11:16 indicates this.

A contextual interpretation of the Abrahamic covenant does not abrogate the human author's grammatical-historical intent of seed, land, and divine\human relationship, but recognizes that those same words allow a fuller and deeper meaning, not always perceived by the human author. Kunjummen, who writes from the context of dispensationalism, agrees saying: "Divine accommodation in the use of human language is not tantamount to divine self-reduction of authorial intent to the understanding of the biblical writer."[29]

---

29. Kunjummen, "Single Intent," 109.

PROGRESSIVE REVELATION

Another issue of hermeneutics that relates to the Abrahamic covenant is that of progressive revelation. John Walvoord in speaking to this issue says: The issue accordingly is not progressive revelation versus nonprogressive revelation, but rather whether in progressive revelation there is contradiction or correction of what was commonly assumed to be the main tenor of Old Testament revelation.[30]

The problem with Walvoord's statement is what is meant by " . . . commonly assumed to be the main tenor of Old Testament revelation." Though this author concurs with Turner that "it appears exceedingly doubtful that the New Testament reinterprets the Old Testament so as to evaporate the plain meaning of its promises,"[31] the argument persists concerning what is meant by "plain meaning."

Daniel Fuller's understanding of progressive revelation is helpful:

> Why could not the Old Testament revelation be thought of as the grain of sand which, after entering the oyster of progressive revelation, has the pearl of additional and deeper concepts added to it without necessarily canceling out the original grain of sand?[32]

Any interpretation of the Abrahamic covenant must take into account the seventy-four references to Abraham in the New Testament and how they interpret and inform the Old Testament text.

Directly related to the issue of progressive revelation are that of prophecy and fulfillment, the use of the Old in the New, and typology. Each of these issues is obviously influenced by the addition of new revelation that speaks to the prophecies and types of the Old Testament and to the way the New Testament understands and interprets the Old. The limited scope of this book will allow only a brief discussion of these issues.

---

30. Walvoord, "Israel's Program," 20.
31. Turner, "Continuity of Scripture," 282
32. Fuller, "Hermeneutics," 233.

Though Pentecost notes the problems of interpreting prophecy,[33] the rules stated for correct interpretation are once again restricted by limiting any interpretation to a grammatical-historical interpretation.[34]

Contrariwise, Joel B. Green argues that those who seek literal and detailed fulfillments of Old Testament prophecy " . . . must face the reality that fulfillment is often not quite what was anticipated.[35] He explains:

> When fulfillment exceeds promise, three things are underscored: God's freedom and creativity and the historical quality of biblical prophecy. Given in particular, historical circumstances, prophecy uses words and ideas appropriate to its day. A different historical situation at the time of fulfillment, however, may involve a realization in updated terms beyond the literal meaning of the original prediction.[36]

Dispensationalists, as represented by Charles L. Feinberg, would disagree with Green and instead affirm that "in the interpretation of prophecy that has not yet been fulfilled, those prophecies that have been fulfilled are to form the pattern."[37] Contrariwise, Vern Poythress in his critique of dispensational hermeneutics adequately demonstrates that "pre-eschatological prophetic fulfillments have a hermeneutically different character than do eschatological fulfillments."[38]

The sometime enigmatic nature of prophecy should solicit humility and tentativeness in assertions regarding its fulfillment. For example, Odendaal in his discussion of Isaiah 40–66 notes that those chapters offer an eschatological fulfillment of the Abrahamic covenant.[39] In regard to the fulfillment of that passage he

---

33. Pentecost, *Things to Come*, 45–59.

34. Pentecost, *Things to Come*, 59.

35. Green, *Read Prophecy*, 103.

36. Green, *Read Prophecy*, 104.

37. Feinberg, *Millennialism*, 41.

38. Poythress, *Dispensationalists*, 105.

39. Odendaal, "Eschatological Expectation," 265.

reservedly concludes that " . . . it is evident that neither a purely spiritual nor a purely literal explanation can fathom the fullness of the prophetic proclamation."[40]

Also related to the issue of progressive revelation are the issues of typology and the use of the Old Testament in the New. Again, it is not the scope of this book to fully develop these issues, but rather to note how they relate to the interpretation of the Abrahamic covenant.

Specifically, does the word "land" have any typological significance? Douglas Moo suggests that "typology is best viewed as a specific form of the larger 'promise-fulfillment' scheme that provides the essential framework within which the relationship of the testaments must be understood."[41] He maintains:

> The two Testaments are bound together by their common witness to the unfolding revelation of God's character, purpose, and plan. But the salvation wrought by God through Christ is the fulfillment of 'Old Testament' history, law, and prophecy.[42]

For example, Hebrews 3:7–4:8 employs a typological significance of "land." Based on the pattern of Psalm 95, throughout the passage the word "land" is replaced with the word "rest." It is significant that in the patriarchal promises, "rest" is never used to describe the land. "Rest" is introduced once positively in Deuteronomy to describe the land as "inheritance" (Deut 12:9), and once in a warning passage that disobedience would result in ". . . they will not enter my rest" (Ps 95:11).

Interestingly, the Psalmist chooses "rest" to describe life in the land. The writer of Hebrews picks up on this and takes it a step further. Employing the same word from the Septuagint "rest," he refers to the present and ultimate blessing of being in Christ as one of "rest."

40. Odendaal, "Eschatological Expectation," 274.

41. Moo, "Sensus Plenior," 196.

42. Moo, "Sensus Plenior," 196.

"Rest" in the "land" anticipated "rest" in Jesus Christ. This rest is semi-realized in the believer's present experience in Christ (Heb 4:3), yet it awaits a more consummate fulfillment (Heb 4:9). Moo perceptively concludes "that God had so ordered Old Testament history that it prefigures and anticipates His climatic redemptive acts and that the New Testament is the inspired record of those redemptive acts.[43]

One other issue that relates to progressive revelation is the thorny issue of the use of the Old Testament in the New. This author would suggest the "canonical approach" to that issue wherein "any specific biblical text can be interpreted in light of its ultimate literary context—the whole canon, which receives its unity from the single divine author of the whole" (Moo 1986, 205). Moo offers four commendations of the canonical approach:

> (1) it builds on the scripturally sound basis of a redemptive-historical framework, in which the Old Testament as a whole points forward to, anticipates, and prefigures Christ and the church; (2) this scheme can be shown to have its antecedents in what the Old Testament itself does with earlier revelation; (3) the questionable division between the intent of the human author and that of the divine author in a given text is decreased; (4) the 'fuller sense' discovered by Jesus and the apostles in Old Testament texts is, at least to some extent, open to verification.[44]

When applied to the Abrahamic covenant, the canonical approach enriches and expands the interpretation of it, freeing it from its purely ethnic, national, and geographical bonds.

Remember that Jesus Christ is God's Word for these last days. The Old Testament anticipated and foreshadowed Him, while the NT offers us a full revelation of Him. The following texts remind us that the OT is the word of God about Jesus Christ.

> 25 He said to them, "How foolish you are, and how slow of heart to believe all that the prophets have spoken! 26

43. Moo, "Sensus Plenior," 198.
44. Moo, "Sensus Plenior," 205–6.

> Did not the Christ have to suffer these things and then enter his glory?" 27 And beginning with Moses and all the Prophets, he explained to them what was said in all the Scriptures concerning himself (Luke 24:25–7)

> 44 He said to them, "This is what I told you while I was still with you: Everything must be fulfilled that is written about me in the Law of Moses, the Prophets and the Psalms." 45 Then he opened their minds so they could understand the Scriptures. 46 He told them, "This is what is written: The Christ will suffer and rise from the dead on the third day, 47 and repentance and forgiveness of sins will be preached in his name to all nations, beginning at Jerusalem (Luke 24:44–7).

> 39 You diligently study the Scriptures because you think that by them you possess eternal life. These are the Scriptures that testify about me, 40 yet you refuse to come to me to have life (John 5:39–40).

The words of Jesus Christ lead us to conclude that the OT is "progressive, redemptive revelation. It is revelation because in it God makes himself known. It is redemptive because God reveals himself in the act of redeeming us. It is progressive because God makes himself and his purposes known by stages until the full light is revealed in Jesus Christ."[45]

This progressive, redemptive revelation of Jesus Christ is given through historical events, people, promises, institutions, Christophanies, etc., all of which in some way anticipate or foreshadow the final and full revelation in Jesus Christ.

Goldsworthy sums up the relationship of Jesus Christ to the OT:

> The New Testament emphasizes the historic person of Christ and what he did for us, through faith, to become the friends of God. The emphasis is also on him as the one who sums up and brings to their fitting climax all the promises and expectations raised in the Old Testament. There is a priority of order here, which we must take

45. Goldsworthy, *According to Plan*, 72.

into account if we are to understand the Bible correctly. It is the gospel event, as that which brings about faith in the people of God, that will motivate, direct, pattern, and empower the life of the Christian community. So we start from the gospel and move to an understanding of Christian living, and the final goal toward which we are moving.

Again, we start from the gospel and move back into the Old Testament to see what lies behind the person and work of Christ. The Old Testament is not completely superseded by the gospel, for that would make it irrelevant to us. It helps us understand the gospel by showing us the origins and meanings of the various ideas and special words used to describe Christ and his works in the New Testament. Yet we must also recognize that Christ is God's fullest and final Word to mankind. As such he reveals to us the final meaning of the Old Testament.[46]

There are many studies that show the relationship of Christ to the Old Testament. An older two-volume study by E.W. Hengstenberg, *Christology of the Old Testament*, was written in 1854. This is a scholarly and detailed study (1400 pages) of Old Testament texts showing the prefiguring and prophecy of Jesus Christ in the Old Testament. A more recent study (1991) by Vern Poythress of Westminster Seminary, *The Shadow of Christ in the Law of Moses*, details how Christ is prefigured in the Pentateuch (5 books of Moses). A look at some of his chapter titles shows how starting with Christ and moving back into the Old Testament gives us insight into a fuller meaning of Christ.

1. The Tabernacle of Moses: Prefiguring God's Presence through Christ

2. The Sacrifices: Prefiguring the Final Sacrifice of Christ

3. The Priests and the People: Prefiguring Christ's Relation to His People

4. General Principles for God's Dwelling with Human Beings: Prefiguring Union with Christ.

46. Goldsworthy, *According to Plan*, 106–107.

5. The Land of Palestine, the Promised Land: Prefiguring Christ's Renewal and Dominion over the Earth.

6. The Law and Its Order: Prefiguring the Righteousness of Christ

7. The Purpose of the Tabernacle, the Law, and the Promised Land: Pointing Forward to Christ

8. The Punishments and Penalties of the Law: Prefiguring the Destruction of Sin and Guilt Through Christ

9. False Worship, Holy War, and Penal Substitution: Prefiguring the Spiritual Warfare of Christ and His Church.[47]

It should be clear that Jesus Christ is the key to both the Old and New Testaments. We conclude this section with the words of Goldsworthy:

> In order to know how any given part of the Bible relates to us, we must answer two prior questions: how does the text in question relate to Christ, and how do we relate to Christ? Since Christ is the truth, God's final and fullest word to mankind, all other words of the Bible are given their final meaning in him. The same Christ gives us our meaning and defines the significance of our existence in terms of our relationship to him.[48]

THE READERS' CONTEXT

One final issue relating to the understanding of the Abrahamic covenant is the influence of one's own context on his interpretation of the text. Within the reader's own context there are several considerations that influence the interpretation of the text. All interpreters approach the text with an already existing worldview and pre-understanding. A self-consciousness of this pre-existing worldview, along with a willingness to subject it to possible reformation under the authority of the text are essential for relevant and authoritative interpretation.

47. Poythress, *Shadow of Christ,* vii–ix.

48. Goldsworthy, *According to Plan,* 91.

Also, there must be a consciousness of the actuality that the world of the Bible and the world of subsequent readers are changed worlds. The interpreter must look for legitimate correspondences between his world and the world of the Bible and beware of making illegitimate correspondences. The interpreter must also be aware that in his contemporary world there exists a gap, not only between his culture and that of the Bible, but also between cultures within his own world. This self-awareness of cultural gap will serve as a check on undue outside influence being brought to the text.

A SUMMARY CRITIQUE OF DISPENSATIONAL INTERPRETATION OF THE ABRAHAMIC COVENANT

Purpose

Dispensationalism is presently undergoing modification. The direction in which contemporary dispensationalists are moving is encouraging, as is the similar movement in covenant theology. There appears to be much less fixation to a "system," and much more attention to exegesis, biblical theology, and the issues of hermeneutics. This present willingness to discuss differences with other schools of interpretation[49] indicates an admission that those who, though they adhere to the authority of Scripture, interpret Scripture differently are not enemies of the cross.

This summary critique is designed to clarify some of the issues regarding the interpretation of the Abrahamic Covenant that need to be addressed so that Dispensationalism can continue to be transformed into a "system" that is thoroughly and defensibly biblical.

---

49. Feinberg, *Continuity and Discontinuity*; Blaising and Bock, *Dispensationalism, Israel, and the Church*, Saucy, "Israel and the Church."

The Issue of Biblical Context

The failure to explicate the relationship of Genesis 12:1–3 to the first eleven chapters of the Bible is one of the most serious flaws of Dispensationalism. This disassociation of the Abrahamic covenant from God's primal intentions for the world results in a multi-track approach to the Bible. In classic Dispensationalism it appears that God began with a plan for all humanity and then, beginning with Genesis 12, He switched tracks and began a new plan for only a segment of humanity, Israel. And, this new plan is only remotely related to what God intended in the original creation.

It is unfortunate that in Eugene Merrill's history of Israel, that connection is not fully developed. He states in regard to the Torah:

> [The Torah] . . . is a theological treatise whose purpose is to show that God the Creator will, through an elect nation Israel, sovereignly achieve his creative and redemptive purposes for all mankind.[50]

Though Merrill notes the above purpose in relation to the Torah, he totally neglects to discuss the Abrahamic covenant in the nineteen pages given to the Abrahamic history.[51]

David J. A. Clines in his discussion of the relationship of Genesis 1–11 and the patriarchal history shows that the goal of the Shem genealogy (11:10–26) is Abraham, and that the genealogy of Abraham (11:26–30) serves as a link between the primeval history and the patriarchal history.[52] Perhaps one of the most cogent discussions of the relationship of the Abrahamic covenant to Genesis 1–11 is given by William J. Dumbrell.[53] He summarizes that relationship saying:

> Gen. 12:1–3 is the rejoinder to the consequences of the fall and aims at the restoration of the purposes of God for the world to which Gen. 1–2 directed our attention.

50. Merrill, *Kingdome of Priests*, 25.

51. Merrill, *Kingdome of Priests*, 25–43.

52. Clines, *Pentateuch*, 78.

53. Dumbrell, *Covenant and Creation*, 47–79.

> What is being offered in these few verses is a theological blueprint for the redemptive history of the world, now set in train by the call of Abraham.[54]

Observing the connection between Genesis 12:1–2 and Genesis 1–11 yields not only the fruit of observing more unity in the purposes of God, but also a recognition of the universal scope of the terms of the Abrahamic covenant. Based on that connection the Abrahamic covenant is loosed from the bonds of ethnicity and nationality and is liberated to address all believing peoples and the entire creation.

More attention needs to be given to the placement of the Abrahamic covenant in its biblical context and how that context nuances its understanding.

THE ACTUAL TERMS OF THE COVENANT

The Seed of Abraham

When viewed against the backdrop of Genesis 1–11 and in light of the New Testament, the features of the Abrahamic covenant are infused with deeper hues that solicit attraction from more than just the physical descendants of Abraham. The inclination of earlier forms of Dispensationalism was to exclude Gentiles from all but the soteriological benefits of this covenant. In so doing, they incited envy for the privileges that Israelites had, yet offered no hope for Gentile participation in those privileges.

Classic dispensationalists affirmed discontinuity in the redemptive program of God based upon their distinction of an earthly and a heavenly people. Though allowing for the redemption of Gentiles through their connection with Christ, the seed of Abraham, they maintained that New Testament believers were the seed of Abraham only in their participation of the gospel. The other features of the Abrahamic covenant were reserved for the

---

54. Dumbrell, *Covenant and Creation*, 66.

physical descendants of Abraham. They retained the distinction of an earthly and heavenly people.

In classic Dispensationalism, Gentiles are granted status as the seed of Abraham only in the sense that they are blessed in experiencing salvation through Jesus Christ, the seed of Abraham. They are excluded from those promises that are allegedly given to the physical seed.[55] Gentiles are "seed" in one sense, but they are not in another. They are "seed" in redemption but not "seed" in eschatology.

Classic Dispensationalism ends up with two seeds of Abraham, even though Galatians 3:16 teaches that the one seed of Abraham is gathered together in Christ. Contrariwise, Progressive Dispensationalists no longer maintain such discontinuity in redemption but see "one people of God, saved by grace through faith in the promises of God based on the atoning death of Christ."[56] The earthly\heavenly dichotomy is erased.[57]

This admission of "one people of God" in redemption needs to be investigated further. For, if it is conceded that there is but one people of God in redemption, then can there not be one people of God in eschatology? Progressive Dispensationalism more clearly delineates the redemptive continuity that exists between Israel and the church as the seed of Abraham[58] yet it remains reluctant to apply that continuity to its fullest limits in regard to eschatology.

Admittedly, Progressive Dispensationalists do recognize that both Israel and the church share a common ultimate destiny in the city of God.[59] In this regard there is eschatological continuity; however, maintaining the distinction that Israel is "a nation among nations" and that the church is "formed from all nations,"[60] seems not only to contradict passages such as 1 Peter 2:9, but also bifurcates the destinies of Israel and the church.

55. Walvoord, "Abrahamic Covenant," 421.

56. Breshears, "Response to Craig Blaising," 3.

57. Saucy, "Israel and the Church," 241.

58. Breshears, "Response to Craig Blaising," 3.

59. Blaising, "Developing Dispensationalism," 277.

60. Saucy, "Israel and the Church," 252; 258.

This designation of Israel as "a nation among nations" fails again to recognize the Genesis 1–11 backdrop for the covenant and consequently fails to see that national Israel in its time was the vehicle of God through which the nations were to be reached. Admittedly, the geo-political status of Israel is an issue of the Abrahamic covenant. By use of the term *goy in* Gen 12:2, Israel is designated as a nation, a political entity, like the *goyim,* the other nations of the world.

However, it is not Israel solely in her ethnic, national status alone that is to expect the kingdom of God on earth, but rather Israel as the people of God, who by faith enter into God's covenant with Abraham, including all subsequent believers who are ingrafted into the olive tree.

As noted earlier, Peter used the terms describing Israel's unique position (1 Pet 2:9) to refer to the church. The church is now a "nation." This is the Greek word used to translate "nation" in the Septuagint.

This is not to say that national Israel is disenfranchised from the promise, but rather that New Testament believers are incorporated into that privileged position with believing Israelites, because God's nation has intentionally expanded its members and its borders.

The Land

Once again, the backdrop of Genesis 1–11 enhances our understanding of *haaretz.* The very first time *aretz* is mentioned in the Scripture is Genesis 1:1 in the syntagm, "heaven and earth," and the next time in Genesis 1:10 with reference to "the dry land." God's primal intentions for man was that he exercise dominion over *haaretz* (Gen 1:26–27). Due to the fall this dominion would entail struggle (Gen 3:17–9); nevertheless, a world-wide responsibility persisted even after the flood (Gen 9:1).

In classic Dispensationalism the promise of land to Abraham is nowhere related to the divine primal intentions for the earth. The gift of land to Abraham is viewed in disassociation from those intentions, being consummated in a Jewish kingdom followed by a restoration of all things.

Darrell Bock, though bringing criticism from other Progressive Dispensationalists, commendably relates the covenants to the kingdom rule of God and also relates New Testament believers to those covenants. He says that "Blessing comes to the audience, not through descent but through turning to the one who has authority to give blessing."[61] In so doing, Bock sees in the church an inauguration of the fulfillment of the covenants of the Old Testament. He says in reference to Acts 3:25–6:

> With the allusion to the Abrahamic covenant, all three of the major covenants have received mention in either Acts 2 or Acts 3. The career of Jesus represents the opportunity for men to share in the fulfillment of all of God's promises, a fulfillment that is presented as a package. The promises of God and His kingdom program are both 'already-not yet,' as well as 'unity in diversity.'[62]

Bock also sees a consummate fulfillment in a kingdom age "when God brings the program of His rule to completion."[63] This author agrees with David Turner's and Stephen Spencer's recognition:

> Bock's essay amounts to a helpful synthesis of the best insights of covenant theologians on present eschatology with the dispensationalists view of the future response of national Israel to the gospel.[64]

I recommend viewing the Abrahamic promise of land against the backdrop of Genesis 1–11. From that perspective, believing descendants of Abraham, as well as proselytes, were to enjoy occupation of that land of Palestine and all that entailed spiritually, as a microcosmic participation in the kingdom rule of God. This kingdom rule is presently experienced in the church, as a semi-realized

---

61. Bock, "The Reign of the Lord Christ," 14.

62. Bock, "The Reign of the Lord Christ," 14.

63. Bock, 1987, 14.

64. Turner and Spencer, Response to Darrell Bock, 1987, 1.

eschatological fulfillment of the covenants, and awaits a future consummate fulfillment in the geo-political kingdom of God in the eternal kingdom.

The classic dispensational view of the purely national nature of the land promise and its fulfillment in a Jewish kingdom must be rejected on the grounds that it fails to take into account the biblical-historical context of the land promise, the theological significance of that promise, and the paucity of New Testament material directly related to that promise.

Admittedly, Progressive Dispensationalists recognize that a millennial kingdom is but transitory to an eternal kingdom. Blaising says:

> ... the millennium does not properly bear the full climax of history. The goal of the dispensations is not the millennial kingdom but the eternal kingdom. The millennial kingdom is seen more as a temporary, transitional phase of God's kingdom plan . . . .[65]

The moderation within Dispensationalism needs to further examine the promise of land in light of the three aforementioned issues.

NEW TESTAMENT PASSAGES

An unresolved issue that continues to affect the understanding of the nation of Israel's role in the future as well as the other terms of the Abrahamic covenant is the paucity of New Testament material that speaks with the clarity of the Old Testament to Israel's future land inheritance. For instance, Kaiser, in giving a biblical-historical view of the Promised Land, adequately from an Old Testament basis builds a case for Israel's future possession of Palestine.[66]

However, when he come to Romans 9–11, which he calls "the most significant passage on this subject in the New Testament,"[67] though establishing this text as a "blunt witness to God's everlasting

---

65. Blaising, "Developing Dispensationalism," 268–69.

66. Kaiser, *Old Testament Theology*, 302–9.

67. Kaiser, *Old Testament Theology*, 310.

work on behalf of Israel,"[68] he fails to demonstrate his assertion that "the main lines of Paul's argument in Romans 9–11 are clear and in complete agreement with the promise of the land to the nation of Israel in the Old Testament."[69]

Admittedly, an argument from silence neither affirms nor negates the promise of the Old Testament, but raises the question as to whether or not they are to be understood in a fuller way.

As noted earlier, the seventy-four references to Abraham in the New Testament fail to affirm the features of the covenant as "literally" understood in the Old Testament. Rather, the most significant features highlighted in the New Testament concerning Abraham were the faith relationship that he enjoyed with God and the realization that Jesus Christ, as the supreme representative seed of Abraham, is both the guarantor and inheritor of those promises. The conclusion of Bruce Waltke, a former Dispensationalist, concerning the absence in the New Testament of any mention of an earthly reign of Christ before His appearing[70] needs a more convincing response than that given by Walter Kaiser.[71] I would suggest that the historical-grammatical meaning of the "land promise" is not emasculated by the "fuller sense" of the New Testament but rather enriches and expands that sense.

HERMENEUTICAL ISSUES

The *sine qua non*

Ryrie's three *sine qua non*[72] are no longer the basis of Dispensationalism. Two of three that formerly most affected the issue of hermeneutics have been reduced by Progressive dispensationalists to one, i.e., the distinction between Israel and the Church.[73]

---

68. Kaiser, *Old Testament Theology*, 310.

69. Kaiser, *Old Testament Theology*, 310.

70. Waltke, "Kingdom Promises," 273.

71. Kaiser, *Old Testament Theology*, 289–307.

72. Ryrie, *Dispensationalism Today*, 43–47.

73. Bailey, "Dispensational Definitions," 23.

Though the historical and eschatological distinctions between Israel and the Church are perceived differently among dispensationalists, the distinction yet remains. That distinction appears to inhere in the "national" status of Israel.[74]

Though this author does not necessarily disagree with a form of discontinuity between Israel and the church in history and destiny, he fails to see the reasoning for asserting a soteriological continuity and retaining a strict eschatological discontinuity. To allow that the concept of "nation" has been expanded to include the church (1 Pet 2:9) does not obliterate God's intentions for Israel, it merely enlarges them. Does God have two "peoples" through which he accomplishes His plan of world redemption? Would the occupation of the new cosmos, including Palestine, by the people of God be construed as an abrogation of His promise to Abraham? Would the joint-rule of Jew and Gentile believers over all creation fail to meet the intent of Old Testament promises?

In my estimation, the distinction between Israel and the Church as the *sine qua non* of Dispensationalism lacks clarity. The *sine qua non* of Dispensationalism would more clearly be stated as "a commitment to the earthly fulfillment of the land promise to national, ethnic Israel which is uniquely the 'seed' of Abraham with reference to the future fulfillment of the covenants of promise." This commitment is arrived at through their limited understanding of grammatical-historical interpretation.

Grammatical-historical Interpretation

Classic Dispensationalism has a self-imposed restriction on understanding the text of the Bible. By limiting a text's meaning to its grammatical-historical interpretation they rule out any nuances that may be added by further revelation. David Turner rightly recognizes:

> It seems to me that we dispensationalists have the most to lose from a *sensus plenior*, NT reinterprets OT,

74. Saucy, "Israel and the Church," 255.

> hermeneutic. We have the most to gain from an approach
> to progressive revelation which emphasizes informing
> antecedent theology.[75]

The issue of grammatical-historical interpretation is integrally related to the issues of authorial intent and progressive revelation, and it ultimately influences how one understands the related issues of typology, prophecy-fulfillment, and the use of the Old Testament in the New Testament.

As noted earlier, the grammatical-historical approach to Scripture is necessary and adequate as a starting point. However, it falls short due to the now enlarged context of Scripture. It is precisely because of the dual authorship of Scripture (Divine/Human) that the grammatical-historical meaning of Scripture can be developed and expanded. Progressive revelation enlarges on the divine intent in Scripture without emasculating the human author's intent. At the same time progressive revelation may unfold at times an understanding of the human author's intent that may not have been immediately perceptible from the text itself.

A concession that God, the divine author, could have intended more than the physical descendants of Abraham by the term, is one that is confirmed by the New Testament (Gal 3:16, 29). Recognizing that Abraham, the human recipient of the promise, had an understanding of "land" that went beyond the geography of Palestine is likewise confirmed by the New Testament (Heb 11:10, 16, 39, 40). The question is whether these added meanings in any way annul the grammatical-historical meaning.

Classic dispensationalists tended to approach the Abrahamic covenant in a "woodenly" literal way. There seemed to be little development of the typological significance of land (Heb 3: 4). However, even accepting Waltke's affirmation that "the striking correspondences between the land and Christ suggest the sworn-land is a type of the kingdom of God embodied in Christ"[76] does not absolutely rule out the possibility of a future earthly kingdom that serves as a final earthly type of the perfect rest to be

75. Turner, "Continuity of Scripture," 2.

76. Waltke, "Kingdom Promises," 277.

experienced in Christ in the eternal state. As long as this earthly order exists there may be types that foreshadow the heavenly and eternal original.

The interpretation of prophecy is also directly affected by how one handles the issues of authorial intent and progressive revelation. The dispensational approach to prophecy has traditionally been a straight-forward approach that gave little or no attention to the eschatological fulfillment taking place in the church today. However, that is changing. There is much similarity between Bock's inaugural and consummate fulfillment scheme[77] and Robertson's fuller and consummate realizations,[78] even though Bock's ends in the millennium and Robertson's ends in the new creation.

A recognition of partial fulfillment of Old Testament prophecies in the church today is a giant step for dispensationalism. It is an admission that in the progress of revelation, the New Testament does inform the Old Testament, and elicits an understanding that goes beyond the historical-grammatical interpretation.

I recognize three possible conclusions concerning the issue of the eschatological fulfillment of the Abrahamic covenant: (1) the nation of Israel awaits a distinct eschatological fulfillment of the promise to Abraham, while the church participates only soteriologically in the promise to Abraham; (2) the church fulfills the promise to Abraham; (3) the church is ingrafted into Israel and enjoys with believing Jews a present semi-realized fulfillment and awaits a future expanded fulfillment of the Abrahamic covenant.

The current progress in hermeneutics is bound to bring further modifications to both covenantal and dispensational approaches of interpreting Scripture. As development takes place, may it do so heeding Craig Blaising's answers to his own question: "How can a positive contribution be made toward proper development of doctrine?" He answers:

1. Expect orthodox doctrine to develop.

77. Bock, "The Reign," 1–16.
78. Robertson, "Gen 15:6," 288–89.

2. Encourage proper theological method, including interaction and integration from various sources.

3. Encourage the exegetical study of Scripture and the consideration of hermeneutical conclusions that may vary from the existing pattern of doctrine. The tension between doctrine and exegesis may be the catalyst for proper doctrinal development or for further exegetical development which may or may not result in doctrinal development.

4. Locate the continuity center of tradition in Scripture, God's Word, rather than in some past theological expression, a human word. In this way the priority of Scripture over tradition will be maintained.[79]

THE UNITY OF THE COVENANTS

David Turner recommended that "dispensationalists should also rethink the biblical covenants in order to revise the traditional conditional\unconditional scheme."[80] I concur with Turner and would like to take it a step further. Dispensationalism needs to rethink the purpose of the covenants, the recipients, the interrelationship of the covenants, and their fulfillment.

It is unfortunate that most of the dispensational discussion of the covenants themselves is contained in a polemic against covenant theology and fails to explicate how dispensationalists view the covenants. The importance of the Abrahamic covenant is seen largely as "crucial in its evidence regarding God's purposes for Israel."[81] According to classic dispensationalists, the covenants concern the physical descendants of Abraham only.

The failure to see the Abrahamic covenant in relationship to God's primal intentions and the failure to see covenant as the

---

79. Blaising, "Developing Dispensationalism," 130–40.

80. Turner, "Continuity of Scripture," 2.

81. Walvoord, "Abrahamic Covenant," 27.

means by which God binds Himself to both Old Testament and New Testament believers will continue to result in a bifurcation of the purposes of God, the people of God, and of the two testaments.

Even though Progressive Dispensationalism has conceded more unity in the people of God and between the testament, a study of the covenants in relationship to God's primal intentions[82] would yield more continuity.

Though Progressive Dispensationalism accepts a "one people of God" approach in soteriology and accepts a semi-realized eschatological fulfillment of Old Testament prophecy in the Church today, they still have not broken loose completely from bold but unfortunate statements such as this one by Dwight Pentecost:

> Finally, these covenants were made with a covenant people, Israel. In Romans 9:4 Paul states that the nation of Israel had received covenants from the Lord. In Ephesians 2:11–12 he states, conversely, that the Gentiles have not received any such covenants and consequently do not enjoy covenant relationships with God.[83]

Breshears statement that "the promises and prophecies of redemption come to all who are the single redeemed people of God"[84] needs further thought and development to examine whether the theological basis, upon which they have determined that the single redeemed people of God share the same soteriological benefits, can also be used to establish a fully shared eschatological destiny.

The continued discussion and development in hermeneutics will bring further modification to Dispensationalism. The areas of discussion that will perhaps yield the greatest benefit are (1) a clearer understanding of how the Old Testament is used in the New Testament; (2) an application of "canonical process" to Old Testament texts; (3) further discussion on the nature of typology and the understanding of prophetic texts; (4) a deeper self-awareness of the "baggage" interpreters bring to Scripture coupled with

---

82. Dumbrell, *Covenant and Creation*, 984.

83. Pentecost, *Things to Come*, 69.

84. Breshears, "Response to Craig Blaising," 3.

a willingness to allow exegesis to modify their theological systems; and (5) a greater appreciation for how the final and fullest revelation in Jesus Christ determines our understanding of the Old Testament promises.

Chapter 4

Selected New Testament Texts Relating to the Abrahamic Covenant

ROMANS 4

In this chapter the apostle continues his argument that justification is by faith alone. It is faith, not rite or law that establishes man in relationship to God. He illustrates from the experience of Abraham to whom justification was granted prior to the requirement of the rite of circumcision. The apostle contends that circumcision was not the link between Abraham and those who participated in the covenant with him, but rather "faith" was that link (Rom 4:9–12). Circumcision merely portrayed that faith.

He further asserts that Abraham received the promise by faith prior to the giving of the law (Rom 4:13–15). Paul here understands the Abrahamic promise as primarily having redemptive significance.

His conclusion is that the promise comes by faith and that those who share Abraham's faith are related to the promise. "He is the father of us all" and the promise is "guaranteed to all Abraham's offspring" (Rom 4:16).

In quoting Genesis 17:3 Paul equates the Gentile believers of Rome with the "many nations" of the Abrahamic covenant. Both Genesis 17 and Romans 4 make no distinction between the "many nations" and the "seed of Abraham." Abraham is the father of both. Romans 4 shows that Genesis 17 anticipated that "seed of Abraham" and "many nations" involved, not physical descendance, but a relationship of faith.

ROMANS 9-11

This passage is critical to any interpretation of the Abrahamic covenant because it concerns the apparent failure of the covenant promises to the nation of Israel. The apostle's explanation of God's past, present, and future relation to Israel sheds light on the intent and scope of the Abrahamic covenant.

In brief, Romans 9 dispels the notion that physical descendance constitutes Israel as the people of God and clarifies the true nature of that people. Using both the choice of Isaac over Ishmael in 9:6–9 and the choice of Jacob over Esau in 9:10–13, Paul argues that Abraham's true offspring are the those who inherit the promise (v.8) and that those inheritors of the promise become such through their faith participation (9:30–10:21) in the sovereign plan of God (9:1–21).

God's plan to gather a people for Himself also includes those Gentiles who share that faith response (9:22–26; 10:12–13). This inclusion of Gentiles is not to be perceived as a rejection of ethnic Israel. Though ethnicity in itself does not guarantee participation in the purposes of God, God's present extension of His grace to the nations does not exclude the availability of His grace to ethnic Israel (11:1).

The salvation of any Israelite, such as Paul (11:1–2), Elijah (11:2–6), or Jews today, demonstrates God's faithfulness to His promises to ethnic Israel. God's present abrogation of Israel's favored nation status and His glorious work among the nations, serve the dual purpose of saving Gentiles and arousing envy in Israelites.

However, the present extension of God's mercy to the Gentiles should not be construed as a negation of His promises for Israelites.[1] The partial hardening of Jews and the fullness of the Gentiles is the manner[2] in which God is accomplishing the saving of Israel. This is consistent with the Scripture that anticipated the coming of the Deliverer to Zion to take away sins. The Deliverer has come and is now gathering both Jew and Gentile unto Himself (11:25–27). Martin Wouldstra argues that the "saving of all Israel" in Romans 9 is presently being accomplished through the formation into one body of both Jew and Gentile and that Israel " . . . will not form a separate program or a separate entity next to the church."[3]

The olive tree illustration sets forth the unity and continuity of the people of God. As the ingrafting of Gentiles does not replace the original branches, so the ingrafting of Israelites will not supplant the position of Gentiles.

The apostles understanding of God's past, present, and future work among the nations and Israel coincides with the understanding that "the undeniable center of Old Testament religion lies in the believer's response to the words of the covenant God that He would be Abraham's God and the God of his descendants."[4] Included in those descendants are all those who have faith in Abraham's God.

GALATIANS 3

In the apostle's discussion of the relationship of the law to saving faith, he introduces Abraham as a paradigm of saving faith and inclusion in the promises of God. In the course of his discussion

1. See the discussion of Rom 11:11–32 defending a future for Israel (Andrews, "The Future of Israel.").

2. *houtos* is here used with the sense of "in this way" (Arndt and Gingrich, *A Greek-English Lexicon*, 602). As in its two other occurrences in this chapter (vv.5, 31), it describes the manner in which something takes place.

3. Woudstra, "Israel and the Church", 236–7.

4. Woudstra, "Israel and the Church," 227.

the apostle makes some interpretive statements, based on his understanding of the Genesis passages, that reflect on the Abrahamic covenant. These statements are: (1) "those who believe are children of Abraham" (v.7); (2) "The Scripture foresaw that God would justify the Gentiles by faith, and announced the gospel in advance to Abraham: "All nations will be blessed through you" (v.8); (3) "those who have faith are blessed along with Abraham" (v.9); (4) "He redeemed us in order that the blessing given to Abraham might come to the Gentiles through Jesus Christ" (v.14); (5) "The promises were spoken to Abraham and to his seed. The Scripture does not say 'and to seeds,' meaning many people, but 'and to your seed,' meaning one person, who is Christ" (v.16); (6) "But the Scripture declares that the whole world is a prisoner of sin, so that what was promised, being given through faith in Jesus Christ, might be given to those who believe (v.22)."

Paramount in these verses is the redemptive significance of the Abrahamic covenant as it finds its consummation in the person of Jesus Christ. Christ as the quintessential seed of Abraham is both the guarantor and inheritor of the promises of the covenant. Relationship with Christ, established by emulating the faith of Abraham, guarantee one's participation in the promises of the covenant. It is not the keeping of the law nor physical descendance from Abraham that constitutes one as a child of Abraham, but rather faith in Jesus Christ.

These verses sanction the redemptive nature of the Abrahamic covenant. They confirm that covenant as the unifying factor between Jews and Gentiles and they substantiate the view that there is one people of God of all ages that share the covenants of Scripture which find their consummation in Christ.

Strikingly, Paul perceives redemption in Christ to be the dominant, though probably not exclusive, feature of the Abrahamic covenant. He finds the consummation of the covenant in Christ and participation in the covenant to be predicated on relationship to Christ. Though admittedly an argument from silence, the "earthly" nature of the promises to Abraham appears to be somewhat idealized in Christ. Though not necessarily eviscerating those "earthly" elements of the Abrahamic covenant, it certainly places them in a new light.

EPHESIANS 2:11–22

This pericope offers a contrast between Gentiles apart from Christ (2:12) and Gentiles in Christ (2:13). In delineating that contrast, Paul asserts the unity and continuity of the people of God.

In the past Gentiles were able to participate in the covenants of God only through their identification with the God of Israel and their becoming proselytes of the religion of Israel. The advent of Christ ushered in a marked change in the focus of redemption.

No longer does common participation in the religion of Israel guarantee one's participation in the covenants, but rather common participation in the Lord Jesus Christ (the true Israel?) binds one to the covenants of promise.

Formerly, Gentiles apart from Christ were "excluded from citizenship in Israel and foreigners to the covenants of the promise" (2:12); whereas now, Gentiles in Christ "are no longer foreigners and aliens, but fellow citizens with God's people and members of God's household" (2:19).

The dividing wall (2:14) between Jew and Gentile is destroyed through the person and work of Jesus Christ. A new order has been established, replacing the old and forbidding its reconstruction.

The temple of Judaism is now replaced with a temple composed of Jew and Gentile sharing alike the life of the Spirit (2:21–2). Paul interprets the present experience of believing Jews and Gentiles in Christ as that which was anticipated by the covenants.

1 PETER 2:9–10

This text assigns the elevated status granted to Israel in Exodus 19:5–6 to New Testament believers. In unmistakable language, "a chosen people, a royal priesthood, a holy nation, a people belonging to God" (2:9). Peter removes any thought of a continuing distinction between Jew and Gentile, formerly marked by supremacy of the nation of Israel.

Dumbrell cogently discusses the significance of these concepts in their Old Testament context. The Hebrew word for "treasured possession" derives from an Akkadian term which refers "to what is owned personally or what has carefully been put aside for personal use."[5] It is a term that is nuanced by its use in suzerain\vassal relationships.

The Hebrew and Greek words for "kingdom of priests and holy nations" describe the mediatorial function of the nation. In an ancient society the priest was separated from the people in order to serve them. The separation of the people was a demonstration of their allegiance to the covenant. Israel was to serve the world by being distinct from it.

By this new relationship, as disclosed in these terms, Israel is "withdrawn from the sphere of common international contact and finds her point of contact as a nation in her relationship to Yahweh."[6] Under this new constitution she becomes "a societary model for the world. She will provide, under the direct rule which the covenant contemplates, the paradigm of the theocratic rule which is to be the biblical aim of the whole world."[7]

Furthermore, "now, the people of God" (2:10) becomes the designation that Peter grants to New Testament believers, echoing the words of Hosea the prophet (Hos 2:23).

CONCLUSION

The preceding passages share a common perspective of the Abrahamic covenant and of the people of God. In these representative New Testament texts the covenant is largely viewed in light of its redemptive significance. Apart from Romans 11:25–27 a future restoration of the nation of Israel is not even hinted at. Of the

---

5. Dumbrell, *Covenant and Creation*, 85.

6. Dumbrell, *Covenant and Creation*, 87.

7. Dumbrell, *Covenant and Creation*, 87.

seventy-four references to Abraham in the New Testament, not one clearly focuses on the "earthly" elements of the covenant. Even the acceptance of a mass conversion of Israelites at some future time does not demand a return to a former order of things. Due to the advent of Christ, as the seed of Abraham, the New Testament text see a semi-, realized fulfillment of the Abrahamic covenant in New Testament believers.

The texts that consider the question of "who are the people of God?" unequivocally answer "all of those who are in Christ Jesus." In reference to the unity of believing Jews and Gentiles, George N. H. Peters cogently concludes:

> Both elect are the seed, the children of Abraham; both sets of branches are on the same stock, on the same root, on the same olive tree; both constitute the same Israel of God, the members of the same body, fellow-citizens of the same commonwealth; both are Jews 'inwardly' (Romans 2:29), and of the true 'circumcision' (Phil. 3:3), forming the same 'peculiar people,' 'holy nation,' and 'royal priesthood'; both are interested in the same promises, covenants, and kingdom; both inherit and realize the same blessings at the same time.[8]

8. Peters, *Theocratic Kingdom*, 404.

Conclusion

THE MEDIA AND PUBLIC often conclude that being a Christian entails being pro-Israel. A "pro-Israel" stance normally infers that modern day Israel has some sort of divine or biblical right to the land of Palestine, i.e., that ethnic Israelites are the legitimate heirs of the Abrahamic covenant. How did this understanding come about, and is being "pro-Israel" a necessary corollary of biblical Christianity?

Popular American Christian eschatology as represented in books such as the *Left Behind* series, and in prophetic conferences of the last century, and in Dispensationalism emphasized the unique status of Israel among the nations of the world in the plan of God. This plan included the ancient gift of what we know as modern-day Palestine to the Old Testament people of God, known as Israel. Admittedly, if one reads only the Old Testament, he might conclude that Israel is still God's nation and Palestine yet remains a gift and a promise to faithful Jews. However, popular American Christian eschatology does not represent the consensus of Christian theology worldwide nor is it inexorably the position that best reflects biblical understanding.

All Christians must begin their reading of the Bible with the New Testament, without which there is no Christianity. Consequently, Christians as they read the New Testament become aware that the coming of Jesus introduces a fundamental change in regard to how the Old Testament is understood. This is especially true in regard to the Abrahamic covenant.

As Christians we read the Old Testament from the perspective of Christ's teaching that he was the Messiah whom the Old Testament anticipated. The Old Testament was promise; Jesus is fulfillment. Jesus was the only Israelite who truly fulfilled the righteous requirement of the law. He alone was the faithful covenant-keeper. As the quintessential seed of Abraham, he inherited all the promises given to Israel. Now, in light of the fulfillment in Jesus, all believers share His inheritance through their faith in Jesus Christ. Anyone, regardless of ethnicity, can become an inheritor of the Old Testament promises. This is what the New Testament teaches clearly: "If you belong to Christ, then you are Abraham's seed, and heirs according to the promise" (Gal 3:29).

In regard to the current struggle over the land in the Middle East, God's promises to Abraham belong to Jesus Christ and to all believers, Jews and Palestinians included, who have come to faith in Jesus Christ. Jews and Palestinians who continue to reject Jesus as the Messiah are in the same boat spiritually before God. They inherit nothing. Though one or the other may be 'more just' on certain ethical and political issues, neither Jews nor Palestinians are in greater favor with God or have a divine right to the land.

> There is no difference, for all have sinned and fall short of the glory of God, and are justified freely by his grace through the redemption that came by Christ Jesus (Rom 3:22–24).

Does the church of Jesus Christ have a legitimate and biblical basis to lay claim to the covenant given to Abraham? Greg K. Beale[1] and W. J Dumbrell.[2] view the Abrahamic Covenant in relationship to the broader biblical theme of creation/recreation. This context of a creation/recreation motif establishes a "beyond-ethnicity" scope for the Abrahamic Covenant because it views the covenant in relationship to the creation-wide purposes of God.

1. Brower and Elliot *Eschatology in Bible & Theology* 11–52.
2. Dumbrell *Covenant and Creation,* 11–43.

A New Testament understanding of the Abrahamic Covenant fully allows that "faith not ethnicity" defines the descendants of Abraham, and clarifies that New Testament believers are fully the "seed of Abraham." A Christian interpretation of the biblical texts containing the Abrahamic covenant establishes Christ and those in Christ as the legitimate heirs of the promise.

The three giant steps taken by modified dispensationalists and noted in Chapter Two, need to be pursued: (1) the recognition of an "already, not yet" approach to fulfillment of prophecy; (2) the recognition of "one people of God"; and (3) the concession to a continuity of redemption between the testaments.

It appears that it is within the realm of eschatology that dispensationalism retains its distinction. Specifically, this distinction lies in the unique status granted to national Israel and her restoration to the land of Palestine. A number of covenant theologians allow for a fulfillment of "land" for Israel, though they do not so narrowly define the land, nor do they understand Israel in its exclusive ethnic, national sense. Strikingly, even on the issue of a restored Israel there are dispensational and covenant views that approximate each other.

As stated in the third chapter, considering the issues of hermeneutics will yield some of the greatest rewards in a deeper and fuller appreciation of the role of the Abrahamic covenant. Also, giving more attention to the covenants, especially in a biblical-theological study such as Dumbrell[3] and Robertson,[4] will more fully explicate the relationship of the Abrahamic covenant to creation and to Christ.

I have arrived at a position that approximates covenant theology, namely, that the Abrahamic Covenant confirms and explicates the program by which God redeems a people for Himself. It must be recognized that Israel and the church are to be perceived as sub-categories of a larger concept, i.e. the people of God. The Abrahamic covenant is not the beginning of the people of God, but rather God's redemptive means, after the rebellion at Babel and the

---

3. Dumbrell, *Covenant and Creation*.
4. Robertson, *The Christ of the Covenants*.

dispersion, to reclaim a fallen world to Himself. The Abrahamic covenant needs to be viewed in its relation to God's purposes for the entire world, not simply His purposes for a nation. The Abrahamic covenant needs to viewed in light of the inauguration of eschatological times with the first advent of Jesus Christ, as well as the consummation of eschatology at the second advent.

Bibliography

Allis, Oswald T. *Prophecy and the Church*. Phillipsburg: Presbyterian and Reformed, 1978.

Andrews, Robert G. "Romans 11:11–32: The Future of Israel." ThM Theses. WTS, 1982.

Arndt, W. F. and F.W. Gingrich. *A Greek-English Lexicon of the New Testament and other Early Christian Literature*. Chicago: University of Chicago, 1957.

Bailey, Mark. "Dispensational Definitions of Kingdom." A Paper prepared after ETS meeting, 1988.

Berkhof, Louis. *Principles of Biblical Interpretation*. Grand Rapids: Baker, 1950.

Blaising, Craig A. and Darrell L. Bock. "Developing Dispensationalism." *Bibliothecra Sacra*. 145 (1988)133–40; 254–80.

———. *Dispensationalism, Israel, and the Church*. Grand Rapids: Zondervan, 1992.

Bock, Darrell L. "The Reign of the Lord Christ." Evangelical Society National Meeting, 1987.

Brower, Kent E. and Elliot, Mark W. *Eschatology in Bible & Theology*. Downers Grove: Intervarsity Press, 1997, 11–52.

Breshears, Gerry. "Response to Craig Blaising, 'Developing Dispensationalism.'" Evangelical Society National Meeting, 1986.

Clines, David J. A. *The Theme of the Pentateuch*. Sheffield: Sheffield Academic, 1978.

Dumbrell, W. J. *Covenant and Creation*. Nashville: Thomas Nelson, 1984.

Dumbrell, W. J. "The Covenant with Abraham." *Reformed Theological Review* (1982) 41:42–50.

Feinberg, Charles L. *Millennialism: The Two Major Views*. Winona Lake: BMH, 1985.

Feinberg, John. ed. *Continuity and Discontinuity*. Westchester: Crossway, 1988.

Feinberg, Paul D. "The Hermeneutics of Discontinuity." In *Continuity and Discontinuity*, edited by John Feinberg. Westchester, Illinois: Crossway Books, 1988, 109–28.

Fuller, Daniel P. "The Hermeneutics of Dispensationalism." Doctoral Dissertation, Northern Baptist Theological Seminary, 1957.

Bibliography

Fuller, Daniel P. *Gospel and Law. Contrast or Continuum*. Grand Rapids: Eerdmans, 1980.

Gates, M. Halstead. "The Amos Quotation in Acts 15." Unpublished Master's Thesis. Dallas Theological Seminary (1940) 20–22.

Gentry, Kenneth L. "Dispensationalism's Achilles Head." In *Dispensationalism in Transition*. Part One (August 1989) 1–2, Part Two (September 1989) 1–2.

Gentry, Peter J. and Stephen J. Wellum. *Kingdom through Covenant*. Wheaton: Crossway, 2012.

Gilstrap, Michael R. "Dispensationalism's Achilles Heel." In *Dispensationalism in Transition*. Part One (February 1989) 1–2, Part Two (March 1989) 1–2, Part Three (April 1989) 1–2.

———. *Today*. Part One (May 1989) 1–2, Part Two (June 1989) 1–2, Part Three (July 1989) 1–2.

Goldsworthy, Graeme. *According to Plan*. Leicester: Inter-Varsity, 1991.

Green, Joel B. *How to Read Prophecy*. Downers Grove: Inter-Varsity, 1984.

Hoekema, Anthony. *The Bible and the Future*. Grand Rapids: Eerdmans, 1979.

Hughes, P.E. *The Divine Plan for Jew and Gentile*. London: Tyndale, 1949.

Kaiser, Walter C. *Toward an Old Testament Theology*. Grand Rapids: Zondervan, 1978.

———. "The Promised Land: A Biblical-Historical View." *Bibliotheca Sacra*. 138 (Oct-Dec 1981) 302–12.

Klooster, Fred H. "The Kingdom an Interpretive Key." In Taped message from Jubilee Conference. Westminster Theological Seminary, 1979.

———. "The Biblical Method of Salvation: A Case for Continuity." In *Continuity and Discontinuity*, edited by John Feinberg. Westchester: Crossway, 1988, 131–60.

Kunjummen, Raju D. "The Single Intent of Scripture - Critical Examination of a Theological Construct." *Grace Theological Journal*. 7 (Spring 1988) 81–110.

Martens, Elmer. *God's Design: A Focus on Old Testament Theology*. Grand Rapids: Baker, 1981.

McComiskey, Thomas Edward. *Covenant of Promise*. Grand Rapids: Baker, 1985.

Merrill, Eugene. *Kingdom of Priests*. Grand Rapids: Baker, 1987.

Miller Jr., P. D. "Syntax and Theology in Genesis 12:3a." in *Vetus Testametum* 34 (1984) 472–76.

Moo, Douglas. "The Problem of Sensus Plenior." In *Hermeneutics, Authority, and Canon*. Edited by D.A. Carson and John D. Woodbridge, 179–211. Grand Rapids: Zondervan, 1986.

Odendaal, Dirk H. "The Eschatological Expectation of Isaiah 40–66 with Special Reference to Israel and the Nations." Doctoral Dissertation, Westminster Theological Seminary, 1966.

Oswalt, John N. "*barak*." in *Theological Wordbook of the Old Testament*. Chicago: Moody, 1980.

Pentecost, J. Dwight. *Things to Come.* Grand Rapids: Zondervan, 1958.

Peters, G. N. H. *The Theocratic Kingdom.* Vol. 1. Grand Rapids: Kregel, 1952.

Poythress, Vern S. *The Shadow of Christ in the Law of Moses.* Brentwood: Wolgemuth and Hyatt, 1991.

———. *Understanding Dispensationalists.* Grand Rapids: Zondervan, 1987.

Ramm, Bernard. *Protestant Biblical Interpretation.* Grand Rapids: Baker Book House, 1970.

Robertson, O. Palmer. *The Christ of the Covenants.* Phillipsburg, NJ: Presbyterian and Reformed, 1980.

Robertson, O. Palmer. "Genesis 15:6: New Covenant Expositions of an Old Covenant Text. *WTJ* 42 (1980) 259–89.

Ross, Allen P. *Creation and Blessing.* Grand Rapids: Baker, 1988.

Ryrie, Charles Caldwell. *Dispensationalism Today.* Chicago: Moody, 1965.

Saucy, Robert L. "Israel and the Church: A Case for Discontinuity." In *Continuity and Discontinuity.* Edited by John S. Feinberg, 239–59. Westchester, Illinois: Crossway Books, 1988.

———. *The Case for Progressive Dispensationalism.* Grand Rapids: Zondervan, 1993.

Scalise, Charles J. "The 'Sensus Literalis': A Hermeneutical Key to Biblical Exegesis." *Scottish Journal of Theology.* 42 (1989) 45–65.

Scofield, C. I. ed. *The Scofield Bible.* London: Oxford, 1917.

Turner, David L. "The Continuity of Scripture and Eschatology: Key Hermeneutical Issues." *Grace Theological Journal.* 6 (Fall 1985) 275–87.

Turner, David L. and Stephen R. Spencer. A Response to Darrell L. Bock's "The Reign of the Lord Christ." A paper presented at the ETS meeting, 1987.

VanGemeren, Willem. *The Progress of Redemption: The Story of Salvation from Creation to the New Jerusalem.* Grand Rapids: Zondervan, 1988.

Waltke, Bruce. "Kingdom Promises as Spiritual." In *Continuity and Discontinuity*, edited by John S. Feinberg, 263–87. Westchester, Illinois: Crossway Books, 1988.

Waltke, Bruce K. and M. O'Connor. *An Introduction to Biblical Hebrew.* Winona Lake: Eisenbrauns, 1990.

Walvoord, John. "Does the Church Fulfill Israel's Program?" *Bibliothecra Sacra.* 137 (January-March 1980) 17–31; (April-June 1980) 118–24.

———. "The Abrahamic Covenant and Premillennialism." *Bibliotheca Sacra.* 108 (Oct-Dec 1951) 414–22.

———. The Fulfillment of the Abrahamic Covenant." *Bibliotheca Sacra.* 108 (Oct-Dec 1945) 27–36.

Wehmeier, Gerhard. "The Theme 'Blessings for the Nations' in Promises to the Patriarchs and in the Prophetical Literature." *Bangalore Theological Forum.* (July-December 1974) 1–13.

Woudstra, Martin. "Israel and the Church: A Case for Continuity." In *Continuity and Discontinuity*, edited by John Feinberg, 221–38. Westchester: Crossway, 1988.

Bibliography

Yarchin, William. "Imperative and Promise in Genesis 12:1–3." *Studies in Biblical Theology.* 10 (Oct 1980), 164–68.

www.ingramcontent.com/pod-product-compliance
Lightning Source LLC
LaVergne TN
LVHW021618080426
835510LV00019B/2634